AF566470

ECONOMIC DEVELOPMENT OF HARYANA

AN ERA OF PROSPERITY

ECONOMIC DEVELOPMENT OF HARYANA

AN ERA OF PROSPERITY

MANDEEP SINGH

and

HARVINDER KAUR

DEEP & DEEP PUBLICATIONS PVT. LTD.

F-159, Rajouri Garden, New Delhi-110027

ECONOMIC DEVELOPMENT OF HARYANA
AN ERA OF PROSPERITY

ISBN 81-7629-558-2

Typeset by S.S. COMPOSERS,
3190, Mohindra Park, Shakur Basti, Delhi-110034.

Printed in India at ELEGANT PRINTERS,
A-38/2, Maya Puri, Phase-I, New Delhi-110064.

Published by DEEP & DEEP PUBLICATIONS PVT. LTD.
F-159, Rajouri Garden, New Delhi-110027.
Phones: 25435369, 25440916
E-mail: ddpbooks@yahoo.co.in • deep98@del3.vsnl.net.in
Showroom:
2/13, Ansari Road, Daryaganj, New Delhi-110002 • Telefax: 23245122

CONTENTS

PREFACE

The name of Haryana instantly conjures up an image of a state which astonishingly combines both—antiquity and plenty. The Vedic land of Haryana has been a cradle of Indian culture and civilization. Replete with myths, legends and Vedic references, Haryana's past is steeped in glory. It was on this soil that *Saint Ved Vyas* wrote *Mahabharata*. It was here 5,000 long years ago that Lord Krishna preached the gospel of duty to Arjuna at the onset of the great battle of Mahabharata "Your right is to do your duty and not to bother about the fruits (outcome) thereof." Since then, this philosophy of the supremacy of duty has become a beacon to succeeding generations.

The history of Haryana is the Saga of the struggle of a *Virile*, righteous, forthright and proud people. From ancient times, the people of Haryana have borne the main brunt of invaders and foreign hordes with their known traits of bravery and valour. They have survived many an upheaval, upholding the traditional glory and greatness of the land to this day. The epoch-making events of the yore, the martyrdom in the First War of Indian Independence in 1857, the great sacrifices in the freedom struggle, and the display of outstanding valour, unflinching courage, and heroism in the recent years are all in keeping with the character of this land of action. Bold in spirit and action, the people of Haryana have formed a bulwark against forces of aggression and anti-nationalism.

Haryana emerged as a separate state in the federal galaxy of Indian Republic on November 1, 1966. With just 1.37% of the total geographical area and less than 2% of Indian population, Haryana has carved a place of distinction for itself during the past three decades. Whether it is agriculture or industry, canal irrigation or rural electrification, Haryana has marched towards modernity with leaps and bounds.

The desire for detailed and analytical study of State of Haryana arose in us as we felt that upto this day mostly Indian economic problems are being studied in academic circles with the comprehensive coverage of the country as a whole and very few studies have been taken to study state economies in depth separately. India is a vast country inhabited by people coming from different racial stocks, professing different religious faiths, having different cultural traditions and possessing different working habits. Climates, conditions, quality of soil and availability of natural resources also vary from region to region. In sphere of economic development too this diversity is very much in evidence. Some are industrialized while in others agriculture is predominant. It is in this perspective that special study of regional economy becomes essential. When the economic problems of the country as a whole are scientifically analysed and statistically observed for proper conclusions, they sometimes do not reflect the problems of the regions which constitute the country and consequently the remedial measures suggested to fight the economic ills are not in accordance with the reality. Therefore, we in this book study the problems of development of Haryana economy in detail and in an analytical manner so that it can help in focusing the attention of policy makers to ground realities of economic development of Haryana, that need to be urgently redressed.

The book comprises of eight chapters dealing practically with all important aspects of development in all the major segments of Haryana's economy. The Chapter 1 provides general introduction of the State of Haryana. It gives an introduction to the history, physiography, soil types, natural resources and climate of the State. An attempt has also been made in this chapter to give a brief profile of all the 19 districts of Haryana.

Chapter 2 deals with an important indicator of economic development, i.e. trends in State Domestic Product at current as well as at constant prices. Distribution of State

Income by Industrial Origin has been analysed in detail. The chapter also attempts to analyse inter state variation in state income of various states of Indian union with specific comparative reference of Haryana.

Chapter 3 investigates the various aspects of human resource development in Haryana. It studies size and growth rate of population, sex composition, age structure, density and rural-urban division of population in state of Haryana. The chapter also studies population policy of the state and attempts of State Government to develop the infrastructure for education and health as an important component of human resource development in the state of Haryana.

Chapter 4 examines the occupational pattern of Haryana's population. The impact of economic development on occupational distribution of Haryana particularly with reference to employment and output aspect has been analysed in detail in this chapter.

Chapter 5 deals with emerging pattern of core sector of Haryana's economy, i.e. agricultural sector. It analyses the development of agriculture in Haryana on the basis of various output and input indicators such as crop pattern, irrigation, use of modern technology, etc. The role of state in agricultural development has also been added in the study of these indicators. Some basic issues related to agricultural development have been highlighted in the end of the chapter.

Chapter 6 deals with emerging pattern of industrial development. It analyses industrial development of Haryana before and after its formation. The chapter covers the study of industrial location, pattern of industrialisation, large scale and medium scale industries, small scale industries in Haryana. Further more, the chapter also analyses the role of State Govt. in industrial development.

Chapter 7 deals with infrastructure facilities which are basic requirements for structural changes and economic development in any economy. The chapter provides development and present status of various constituents of infrastructure such as power, transport, communication, banking, etc.

Chapter 8 makes an attempt to put some recommendations which may go a long way in bringing desired balanced economic development, structural changes and faster growth rate of economy in Haryana.

The book is the result of help and co-operation of many persons. We wish to acknowledge, with a deep sense of gratitude, the diligent guidance, comments, inspiration and encouragement that we received from Dr. K.L. Gupta, Reader, Department of Business Administration, S.K. College, Aligarh. We are extremely thankful to Dr. Amrik Singh, Ex-Principal, G.N. Khalsa College, Yamuna Nagar, Dr. Davinder Singh Dhaliwal, Principal, G.N. Khalsa College, Karnal, Dr. Sukhwant Singh, Head, Department of Commerce, G.N. Khalsa College, Karnal and Dr. J.B. Garg of Mandi Samalakha, for their useful comments and suggestions.

For this book, we have heavily drawn upon the material of several publications, we whole-heartedly acknowledge our debt to authors of these publications. Last, but not the least, we are also grateful to Sh. G.S. Bhatia of Deep and Deep Publications Pvt. Ltd., New Delhi for promptly and so neatly bringing out this publication.

MANDEEP SINGH
HARVINDER KAUR

1

HARYANA ECONOMY: GENERAL INTRODUCTION

I. HARYANA IN HISTORICAL PERSPECTIVE

The present state of Haryana was constituted on November 1, 1966, as a result of the bifurcation of the bilingual state of the Punjab. The state comprises the districts of Gurgaon, Faridabad, Rohtak, Mahindragarh, Hisar, Sirsa, Karnal, Jind, Ambala, Bhiwani, Kurukshetra, Panipat, Sonipat, Jhajjar, Kaithal, Panchkula, Yamuna Nagar, Rewari and Fatehabad—nineteen in all.

The origin of the name of Haryana is traced to different sources and has been explained in several ways. According to one view, 'Haryana' is derived from Hindi word *"Haryali"*, i.e. greenery, which indicates that at one time it was a rich and fertile land. There is another view similar to this, the name originated on account of the fact that this region was at one time covered by *"Haryal-Ban"*, dense forests. Some people trace the origin of the name to Raja Harish Chandra of Oudh, who is said to have first settled in this part of the country. Maharaj Krishan, has suggested that it may have been derived from *"harana"* (robbery) once prevalent in the area.[1] Another writer, G.C. Avasthi, has traced the name back to the Rig Veda itself. According to this writer, Varuraja who ruled over this tract used, 'Haryana' as a qualifying adjective and the areas came to be known as such.[2] Rahul Sanskrityayana, a reputed scholar, held the name to be a corrupt form of *Haridhankya* a term used in ancient literature for this area.[3] Dr. Budh Parkash connects *'Haryana'* with *'Abhirayana'*, as the region was populated by the Ahirs during the post-Mahabharata period,[4] According to Dr. H.R. Gupta, Haryana is a corrupt form of *'Aryana'* the home the Aryans, as *Rajputana* is the land inhabited by the *Rajputs*, *Bhattiana* the abode of *Bhattis*, and *Ludhiana* the habitat of *Lodhis*.[5] This view seems to be more plausible. Similar view is held by some other scholars also. According to eminent historians like A.C. Das, and R.K. Mukherji, the Original home of the Aryan was the region called Haryana. The banks of the fabulous *Saraswati* were their earliest settlements. It was from here that they later migrated to other parts of India, Asia and Europe.

It appears that during the protohistoric period, Haryana was the main centre of the Aryan settlements and the region in all probability, as argued by H.R. Gupta owes its name to this fact.[6]

II. GEOGRAPHICAL PHYSICAL FEATURES

Haryana is located on the north-western side of the Indian union adjoining Delhi. The state extends from 27°3' to 31°9' north latitude, and 74°6' east longitude. On the north it is bounded by the states of Punjab and Himachal Pradesh; on the east by Delhi and Uttar Pradesh and on the south and the west by Rajasthan. Haryana has a total surface area of 44,212 square kilometers and is one of the smallest states of the Indian union.[7]

Physiographically, Haryana can be divided into two distinct regions—the plains and the hills. The plains cover the entire state except the southern part of Mahindragarh district, the south-western part of Gurgaon district and north-eastern part of Panchkula district. The plain can be further sub-divided into eastern and western plains on the basis of aridity. The western plain covers Hisar and Mahindragarh districts and has a higher degree of aridity. This is thirsty land covered by thorny bushes symptomatic of a desert. The unevenness in the surface at places is because of the sand dunes or sand stumps of different sizes or extensions of rocky old hills. The eastern plain extends west of Yamuna river. This plain is remarkably flat and is a rich fertile tract producing a large part of the state's agricultural production. Smoothness of the surface is disturbed by the presence of old banks of abandoned channels of streams which have changed their course frequently. The local relief of the whole plain is insignificant, yet the slope is from northeast to southwest and west except in Bhiwani. In Mahindragarh and Gurgaon the slope is towards the north inhibiting the expansion of irrigation.

The *Aravalli* range is a narrow ridge stretching into Haryana for 90 kms. in the northeast and southwest directions upto Delhi. It covers the southern parts of Mahindragarh and adjoining areas of Gurgaon district. The *Aravalli* range is at no place higher than 518 meters above sea level within Haryana. The ridge area is generally unfavourable to cultivation due to its rocky nature.

There is not a single perennial river passing through Haryana. The Yamuna along with the Punjab rivers is the main source of irrigation water. The Yamuna flows along the eastern boundary of the state. The *Ghaggar,* which is non-perennial, passes through the state and causes considerable damage to agriculture. There are other small rivulets like the *Saraswati, Chautang* and *Sahibi* and its tributaries like *Kanseoti* and the *Indeories* streams. They are mostly dry except during the monsoon, when they cause considerable damage. There is no general drainage problem, but sometimes the floods of *Ghaggar* river and other streams create serious drainage problems locally.

III. CLIMATE AND RAINFALL

The climate of Haryana is of the sub-tropical continential Monsoon type. The annual rainfall in Haryana varies from 25 cms. in Western Hisar district to 110 cms. in Eastern Ambala district. The amount of rainfall increases in the direction from southwest to the northwest of the state. The annual temporal distribution pattern is in the nature of short wet months or weeks and long spells of dry months. There are large variations in the monthly and weekly weather regime from place to place, depending on the distance from the mountains, topographical alignment and location with reference to the *Thar* desert. However, the period from July to September which is the peak precipitation period, accounts for eighty percent of the annual rainfall.[8]

IV. SOIL

Formed almost entirely of alluvium, the state is situated towards the depressions of the rivers *Ganges* and *Indus*. It is a broad level plain standing nearly on the watershed between the basins of the two rivers. It is vast ground of moist land. In the whole of the region except the flood-plains of the Yamuna and *Ghaggar*, the alluvium is of the old type containing sand, clay, silt and hard calcareous concentrations about the size of nuts, known as *'Kankars'*.

In the *Ghaggar* the deposits of the alluvium are of the recent type. They consist of coarse sand and some silt regularly deposited by the rivers and small mountain-streams of the Indo-Gangetic watershed.[9]

In the south-western part; a great deal of wind-blown sand has been piled up in the form of sand dunes. These dunes are sometimes many metres high and extend many kilometers in length. The alluvium is covered by sand making the region as arid and unproductive as a desert.

The only parts useful for cultivation in this region are the places, where due to some reason or other, sand does not collect. Such places are locally called *'Tals'*.[10]

V. HILLY AREAS

There are hardly any hilly tracts in Haryana, except a few in Panchkula and Yamuna Nagar districts—its submontane district—and the range of *Aravalli* chain in the Gurgaon district.

In Panchkula, the hilly areas are generally devoid of vegetation other than rough scrub, and the low bleak hills are little used except as grazing grounds by the *Gujar* population of the area. The tract around *Kalesar* and *Morni*, however, is more valuable. The *Kalesar* area covers about 49 sq. km. in the eastern corner of the Jagadhri Tahsil of Yamuna Nagar District, while the *Morni* tract includes about 65 sq. km. of low hills in the *Shivalik* formation of Panchkula District, which also serves as a connecting link between the Himalayas and the plains.

There are also some high ridges running throughout the tract from the north-west to south-east, with numerous spurs branching out in all directions. These hills are known as the *Morni* (average elevation about 1065 metres) and *Tipra* (elevation about 1370 metres) ranges. In conformation and character, they belong to the outer ranges of the Himalayas. They are separated by the valley of the *Ghaggar* river. The highest point in the tract is the *Karoh* peak (1499 metres) on the *Nahan* border. The whole area differs completely from the rest of the district both in its physical features, its history, and the races of its inhabitants.

In the Gurgaon district, the hill ranges are connected with the great *Aravalli* chain, of which they are among the southernmost spurs. One chain forms the western border of the district from the south-western corner of the *Firozepur* Tahsil, to a point opposite the town of Nuh.[11]

VI. NATURAL RESOURCES

Resources which are freely rendered by nature are known as natural resources. The natural resources of an area include land, water minerals, forests, etc. The level of economic development attained by a country or region depends upon the content and uses of its natural resources. In the words of W.A. Lewis, "Natural resources determine the course of development and constitute the challenge which may not be accepted by the human mind."[12]

The extent of natural resources in Haryana is discussed as under:

(a) Land

Land is considered as the most important of all the natural resources. Land is essential for the habitation of human being and other living creatures. Land is required for agriculture, forest, building road and rail transportation system on its surface. It is not only the size of the geographical area but also its nature and fertility that determines the land endowment of a country.

In Haryana total area according to village papers is 4400 thousand hectares. The land-use in Haryana is shown in Table 1.1.

TABLE 1.1

Classification of Area in Haryana State

Details	*Thousand Hectares*	*Percentage of the Total*
Total Culturable area	3821	86.84%
Land not available for cultivation	464	10.55%
Forest	115	2.61%
Total	4400	100.00%

Source: Director of Land Records, Haryana, Statistical abstract of Haryana, 2000-01; pp. 216-17.

It is clear from the Table 1.1 that out of total land resources 86.84% is total culturable area. Out of this culturable area 219 thousand hectares is fallow land, 50 thousand hectares is uncultivated land excluding fallow land and the net area sown is 3552 thousand hectares. Out of this net sown area, area sown more than once is 2477 thousand hectares. The total cropped area in Haryana is 6029 thousand hectares.[13]

(b) Mineral Resources

Mineral resources are considered as an important variety of non-renewable natural resources on which economic development of the country or state depends. Haryana is not very rich in mineral resources, a great part of it being covered by alluvium. Mineral-bearing tracts are confined to the districts of Mahindragarh and Gurgaon in the south, and to a small narrow belt at the north-western border of Panchkula. The minerals which are known to occur here are limestone, Kankar, Marble, Iron Ore and Slate. Deposits of China clay and Slate are found in Gurgaon and limestone in Ambala. The production of minerals in Haryana is shown in the Table 1.2.

TABLE 1.2

Production of Minerals in Haryana

(Quantity in Metric Tonnes)
(Value in '000 rupees)

Minerals	*1966*		*2000-01*	
	Quantity	*Value*	*Quantity*	*Value*
Kaolin (natural)	5,627	19	30,720	3220
Dolomite	2,613	14	—	—
Limestone	4,92,829	2938	12,422	—
Lime Kankar	3,63,214	603	3000	300
Slate	827	106	—	—
Minor minerals	—	1717	—	14,87,215
Silica Sand	50	1	11,66,584	76,340
Iron ore	—	—	—	63

Source: Indian Bureau of Mines, Nagpur; Statistical abstract of Haryana, 2000-01.

In the state of Haryana minerals are available only in 7 districts of state. These districts include Panipat, Faridabad, Mahindragarh, Ambala, Gurgaon, Rewari and Bhiwani. However, it may be mentioned here that Haryana is a mineral deficient state and moreover the little deposits of minerals that are available in the state are being exploited ruthlessly resulting in decline of mineral production continuously.

(c) Forest Resources

The area under forest in Haryana is very limited. The total area under forests is only 2.6 percent of the total land area. Out of total land area of 44,212 sq. km., the area under forests is just 1149 sq. km. of this total area 59 percent exists only in two districts of Panchkula and Yamuna Nagar.[14]

It must be mentioned here that value of major forests produce in Haryana has shown a remarkable increase. In 1966-67 the total value of timber and firewood production was Rs. 21.49 lakhs which rose to Rs. 25.12 crores in 1999-2000.[15]

VII. PROFILE OF DISTRICTS OF HARYANA

Haryana comprises of 19 Districts, 67 Tahsils, 45 Sub-tahsils, 116 Blocks, 106 Towns and 6995 Villages.[16] The profile of various districts in Haryana is shown in Table 1.3.

TABLE 1.3

District Profile of Haryana

District	*Area (in sq. km.)*	*Total Population (2001)*	*Headquarter*
Ambala	1574	1013660	Ambala
Panchkula	898	469210	Panchkula
Yamuna Nagar	1768	982369	Yamuna Nagar
Kurukshetra	1530	828120	Kurukshetra
Kaithal	2317	945631	Kaithal
Karnal	2538	1274843	Karnal
Panipat	1268	967338	Panipat
Sonipat	2122	1278830	Sonipat
Rohtak	1745	940036	Rohtak
Jhajjar	1834	887392	Jhajjar
Faridabad	2151	2193276	Faridabad
Gurgaon	2766	1657669	Gurgaon
Rewari	1582	764727	Rewari
Mahindragarh	1859	812022	Narnaul
Bhiwani	4778	1424554	Bhiwani
Jind	2702	1189725	Jind
Hisar	3983	1536417	Hisar
Fatehabad	2520	806158	Fatehabad
Sirsa	4277	1111012	Sirsa
Total	44,212	2,10,82,989	Chandigarh

Source: Statistical Abstract of Haryana 2000-01, p. 41.

Table 1.3 show that Bhiwani is the largest district area-wise while the smallest is Panchkula. Population is the maximum in Faridabad and least in Panchkula. The total area of Haryana state is 44,212 sq. km. and total population is 2,10,82,989 in 2001. The capital of Haryana state is Chandigarh. Brief history and administrative structure of various districts is discussed below:

(I) Ambala District

The Ambala district has claims of being one of the historically famous district of Haryana State. The district was explored during British period by A.C. Cunningham and C. Rodgers and later by B.B. Lal and many others. On the basis of various literary and archeological evidences it is possible to give an outline of culture and history of Ambala district. The earliest literary reference to the region comprising the Ambala district exist in the *Taittiriya Aranayaka* which mentions *Turghna* as the bordering region towards the North of Kurukshetra. This locality identified with *Shrughna Sugh* also finds mention in *Panini* (Ancient Indian Literature). It is surmised that Ambala district have been founded by *Amba Rajput* during the 14th century A.D. Another version is that the name is a corruption of *Amba Wala* or the mango-village Judging from mango groves that existed in its immediate neighbourhood. Still another version is that the district has taken its name after goddess "*Bhawani Amba*" whose temple still exists in Ambala city.[17]

The district Ambala lies on the North-Eastern edge of Haryana. It is bounded by the district Yamuna Nagar to the south-east. To its south lies Kurukshetra district while in its west are situated Patiala and Ropar districts of Punjab and the union territory of Chandigarh. The shivalik range of Solan and Sirmaur districts of Himachal Pradesh bounds the Ambala district in the north and the north-east.

The Ambala district has an area of 1568.85 sq. kms. The district comprises of two Sub-divisions, three Tahsils, three Sub-Tahsils and six Blocks. The administrative structure of Ambala District is given in Table 1.4.

The total population of district according to 2001 census is 10,13,660. The population of the district forms 4.8

TABLE 1.4

Administrative Structure of Ambala District

Sub-Division	*Tahsils*	*Sub-Tahsils*	*Block*
(1) Ambala	(1) Ambala	(1) Ambala Cantt.	(1) Ambala—I
(2) Naraingarh	(2) Barara	(2) Mullana	(2) Ambala—II
	(3) Naraingarh	(3) Saha	(3) Barara
			(4) Naraingarh
			(5) Shehzadpur
			(6) Saha

Source: Statistical Abstract of Haryana, 2000-01, p. 17.

percent of total population of Haryana state. The literate population is 6,73,807 out of which 3,90,012 are males and 2,83,795 are females respectively. The sex ratio is 869 and density of population is 644.[18]

The district is mainly drained by non-perennial streams and the drainage system of district comprises of mainly three non-perennial streams.

(a) The Markanda and its tributaries.
(b) The Dangri and its tributaries.
(c) The Ghaggar and its tributaries.

Ambala district is not a mineral rich district. Only limestone is found in some parts of Naraingarh Tahsil.

(2) Panchkula District

Panchkula is the newly formed 17th district of Haryana state. Panchkula is surrounded by Himachal Pradesh in the north, Ambala district in the north-east, Kurukshetra district in east and Union Territory of Chandigarh in the west.

Panchkula has an area of 898 sq. km. It comprises of two Sub-Divisions, two Tahsils, three Sub-Tahsils and four blocks as shown in the Table 1.5.

The total population of the district is 4,69,210. The literate population is 3,09,663 out of which 1,83,859 are males and 1,25,804 are females. The sex ratio is 823 and density of population is 523.[19]

TABLE 1.5

Administrative Structure of Panchkula District

Sub-Divisions	*Tahsils*	*Sub-Tahsils*	*Blocks*
(1) Panchkula	(1) Panchkula	(1) Barwala	(1) Barwala
(2) Kalka	(2) Kalka	(2) Morni	(2) Pinjore
		(3) Raipur Rani	(3) Morni
			(4) Raipur Rani

Source: Statistical Abstract of Haryana, 2000-01, p. 16.

(3) Yamuna Nagar District

Yamuna Nagar district was carved out of district Ambala an October 16, 1989. The district is bounded by the State of Himachal Pradesh in the north, the state of Uttar Pradesh in the east, district of Karnal in south-east, Kurukshetra in the south-west and by Ambala district in the west.

Total area of the district is 1768 sq. km. The district comprises of one sub-division, one Tahsil, four Sub-Tahsils and 6 blocks. The Administrative Structure of the district is shown in Table 1.6.

TABLE 1.6

Administrative Structure of Yamuna Nagar District

Sub-division	*Tahsils*	*Sub-Tahsils*	*Blocks*
(1) Jagadhri	(1) Jagadhri	(1) Bilaspur	(1) Bilaspur
	(2) Chhachrauli	(2) Radaur	(2) Chhachhrauli
		(3) Sadhaura	(3) Jagadhri
		(4) Mustafabad	(4) Radaur
			(5) Sadhaura
			(6) Mustafabad

Source: Statistical Abstract of Haryana, 2000-01, p. 16.

The total population of district according to 2001 census is 9,82,369. The literate population is 3,27,824 out of which 1,98,236 are males and 1,29,588 are females. The sex ratio is 863 while density of population is 556.[20]

(4) Kurukshetra District

The name of Kurukshetra is associated in the *Puranas* and the Great Epic with the legendary king *Kuru* although it appears to be more logical to trace it to the tribe of *Kurus* which was born as a result of merger of the various classes of the Great *Bhartas* who are described in the *Rigveda* as Kindling sacrificial fires on the banks of the sacred *Sarasvati* and *Drishadvati*.

Many geographical names and personalities connected with Kurukshetra occur in the earliest Sanskrit literature and around this region were enacted the opening scenes of the drama of Indian history. Most of the *Vedic* literature was composed here and most of the social, religious and political traditions of this country arose in this region. It is therefore regarded as the cradle of Indian civilization and culture. Kurukshetra shot into prominence as the battle field of *Mahabharta* and as the birth place of the *Holy Gita*. The great 18 day battle of *Mahabharta* was fought here in the ancient past between Kauravas and Pandavas for upholding the cause of *dharma*. It was a war between good and evil, in which the *Pandavas* were victorious. *Bhagvad Gita*, the Song Celestial, is the divine message which was delivered here by *Lord Krishna* to *Arjuna* on the eve of the Great war when he saw the latter wavering from his duty. It epitomises all that is the best and noblest in the Hindu philosophy of life.[21]

The Kurukshetra district has an area of 1530 sq. km. The district comprises of two Sub-divisions, three Tahsils, three Sub-Tahsils and 3 blocks as shown in Table 1.7.

TABLE 1.7

Administrative Structure of Kurukshetra District

Sub-divisions	*Tahsils*	*Sub-Tahsils*	*Blocks*
(1) Thanesar	(1) Thanesar	(1) Ladwa	(1) Ladwa
(2) Pehowa	(2) Pehowa	(2) Ismailabad	(2) Pehowa
	(3) Shahbad	(3) Babain	(3) Shahbad

Source: Statistical Abstract of Haryana, 2000-01, p. 18.

The total population of the district according to 2001 census is 8,28,120. The literate population is 5,00,397 out of which 2,96,947 are males and 2,03,450 are females. The sex ratio is 866 and density of population is 541.[22]

(5) Kaithal District

Without an iota of doubt, the antiquity of Kaithal or *'Kapisthala'* exists. Its antiquity is related to *Vedas* and *Brahmavarta. Kapisthala* in *Yajurveda* is *Kaithal.* Its name is concerned with *Kapi Rishi,* a compiler of *"Yajurveda Katha Samhita."* After its compilation he explained about *Kapisthala* to his pupil community. Its reference is found in Mahabharata and *"Vamana Puran"* also.[23]

District Kaithal of Haryana is situated in the state's north-west direction, its portion of *Gulla Cheeka* falls in the north-west boundary alongwith Siwan, District Patiala of Punjab also touches its boundary.

The Kaithal district has an area of 2317 sq. km. The district comprises of two sub-Divisins, two Tahsils, five sub-Tahsils and five blocks as shown in the Table 1.8.

TABLE 1.8

Administrative Structure of Kaithal District

Sub-divisions	*Tahsils*	*Sub-Tahsils*	*Blocks*
(1) Kaithal	(1) Kaithal	(1) Fatehpur	(1) Guhla at Cheeka
(2) Guhla	(2) Guhla	(2) Kalayat	(2) Kaithal
		(3) Siwan	(3) Pundri
		(4) Rajound	(4) Kalayat
		(5) Dhand	(5) Rajound

Source: Statistical abstract of Haryana, 2000-01, p. 18.

The total population of the district according to 2001 census is 9,45,631. The literate population is 4,78,039 out of which 3,00,486 are males and 1,77,553 are females. The sex ratio is 854 and density of population is 408.[24]

(6) Karnal District

Karnal is one of historical districts of Haryana. It is also known as a city of '*Daanveer Karn*'. It is known all over the world for production of rice, wheat and milk, and agriculture research institutions like NDRI, CSSRI, Wheat Research Directorate, National Bureau of Animal Genetics Research, Sugarcane Breeding Institute, etc.

Karnal is important city on Delhi Ambala Rail Line and Shershah Suri Marg (G.T. Road). It is connected with all important places in the country. It is 123 km. from Delhi and 130 km. from Chandigarh. Karnal district lies on the western bank of river Yamuna which once flowed about 11 km. to the east forming eastern boundary of the district. The Karnal district is surrounded by Kurukshetra district on its north-west, Jind & Kaithal district on its west, Panipat district on its south and Uttar Pradesh on east.

Karnal district has an area of 2538 sq. km. The district comprises of two Sub-Divisions, five Tahsils, three Sub-Tahsils and six Blocks as shown in the Table 1.9.

TABLE 1.9

Administrative Structure of Karnal

Sub-divisions	*Tahsils*	*Sub-Tahsils*	*Blocks*
(1) Karnal	(1) Karnal	(1) Nissing	(1) Gharaunda
(2) Assandh	(2) Assandh	(2) Ballah	(2) Indri
	(3) Nilokheri	(3) Nigdhu	(3) Karnal
	(4) Indri		(4) Nilokheri
	(5) Gharaunda		(5) Nissing
			(6) Assandh

Source: Statistical Abstract of Haryana, 2000-01, p. 17.

The total population of the district according to 2001 census is 12,74,843. The literate population is 7,42,322 out of which 4,45,660 are males and 2,96,662 are females. The sex ratio is 864 and density of population is 506.[25]

(7) Panipat District

District Panipat has a very glorious place in the

history of India. It is said that, at the time of battle of Mahabharat, the five villages were demanded by the *Pandavas* from *Duryoudhana*, "Panpat" was one of them. Later on which was converted to the name of Panipat. This district which is situated 90 km. from Delhi (National Highway Number—1) on 'Shershah Suri Marg' has significant importance in the history. Three major battles were fought here which has converted Indian History a new way. The first battle was fought between Ibrahim Lodhi and Babar in the year 1526 A.D. which resulted to a strong base of *Mugal Samrajya*. The second battle was fought between Akbar and Hemu of Rewari in the year 1556 A.D. and this also led to a strong base of *Mugal Samrajya*. The third battle was fought between Ahmad Shah Abdali and Sardar Sada Shiv Bhau in the year 1761 A.D. wherein the Marathas were defeated.[26]

The district also touches other districts of Haryana, viz. Karnal in north, Jind in west, and Sonipat in south and in east touches with Uttar Pradesh across Yamuna.

The Panipat district has an area of 1268 sq. km. The district comprises of two sub-divisions, three Tahsils, two Sub-Tahsils and five Blocks as shown in the Table 1.10.

TABLE 1.10

Administrative Structure of Panipat District

Sub-divisions	*Tahsils*	*Sub-Tahsils*	*Blocks*
(1) Panipat	(1) Panipat	(1) Bapauli	(1) Panipat
(2) Samalkha	(2) Samalkha	(2) Madlauda	(2) Israna
	(3) Israna		(3) Madlauda
			(4) Samalkha
			(5) Bapauli

Source: Statistical Abstract of Haryana, 2000-01, p. 18.

The total population of the district according to 2001 census is 9,67,338. The literate population is 5,68,476 out of which 3,51,663 are males and 2,16,813 are females. The sex ratio is 830 and density of population is 763.[27]

(8) Sonipat District

Sonipat is situated on the eastern boundary of the state. The district was formed on Sept. 22, 1992. It was carved out of Rohtak district.

Sonipat district has an area of 2122 sq. km. The district comprises of three sub-divisions, four Tahsils and six blocks. The Administrative structure of the district is shown in Table 1.11.

TABLE 1.11

Administrative Structure of District Sonipat

Sub-divisions	*Tahsils*	*Sub-Tahsils*	*Blocks*
Sonipat	Sonipat	—	Gohana
Gohana	Gohana		Kharkhoda
Gohana	Gohana		Rai
	Kharkhoda		Sonipat
			Mundlana
			Kathura

Source: Statistical Abstract of Haryana, 2000-01, p. 19 .

The total population of the district is 1,2,78,830. The literate population is 5,74,125 out of which 3,60,579 are males and 2,13,546 are females. The sex ratio is 839 while density of population is 603.[28]

(9) Rohtak District

The district derives its name from its head quarter's town Rohtak which is said to be a correction of *Rohtashgarh*, a name still applied to the ruined sites (also called *Khokhrakot*) of 2 older sites, one lying immediately north of present town and other about 5 kms. towards the east. Traditionally, it is named after *Raja Rohtash* in whose days city is said to have been built.[29]

The district lies in the south-east of Haryana State. It is bounded by Jind and Sonipat districts on the north, Jhajjar district on the south, Jhajjar and Sonipat districts on the east, Hisar and Bhiwani on the west side.

The district has an area of 1745 sq. km. It comprises of

two Sub-divisions, two Tahsils, two Sub-tahsils and five Blocks as shown in Table 1.12.

TABLE 1.12

Administrative Structure of Rohtak

Sub-divisions	*Tahsils*	*Sub-Tahsils*	*Blocks*
(1) Rohtak	(1) Rohtak	(1) Sampla	(1) Kalanaur
(2) Meham	(2) Meham	(2) Kalanaur	(2) Lakhan
			(3) Majra
			(4) Meham
			(5) Rohtak
			(6) Sampla

Source: Statistical Abstract of Haryana 2001, p. 18.

The total population of the district according to 2001 census is 9,40,036. The literate population is 6,00,453 out of which 3,65,713 are males and 2,34,740 are females. The sex ratio is 847 and density of population is 539.[30]

(10) Faridabad District

Faridabad is famous for its industry not only in India but in whole of Asian continent. The industry of this district satisfy needs not only of India but the goods produced here are exported all over the world. The small and large scale industries located in Faridabad have made it the biggest industrial center of Haryana.

Faridabad district was formed in 1979 but in actual the foundation of its systematic development was laid in 1947 when Faridabad Development Board was set-up under the Chairmanship of Pandit Nehru, the first Prime Minister of India.

Total area of the district is 2151 sq. km. The district comprises of five Sub-divisions, five Tahsils and six Blocks. The administrative structure of the district is shown in Table 1.13.

The total population of the district is 21,93,276. The literate population is 4,61,817 out of which 3,19,072 are males

TABLE 1.13

Administrative Structure of Faridabad District

Sub-divisions	*Tahsils*	*Sub-Tahsils*	*Blocks*
(1) Faridabad	(1) Ballabgarh	—	(1) Ballabgarh
(2) Ballabgarh	(2) Faridabad		(2) Faridabad
(3) Palwal	(3) Palwal		(3) Hathin
(4) Hodel	(4) Hathin		(4) Hodel
(5) Hathin	(5) Hodel		(5) Palwal
			(6) Hassanpur

Source: Statistical Abstract of Haryana, 2000-01, p. 19.

and 1,42,745 are females. The sex ratio is 839 while density of population is 1020.[31]

(11) Gurgaon District

Gurgaon district is situated in National Capital Region (NCR) of Delhi, the capital of India. It is just 10 kms away from Indira Gandhi International Airport, Delhi. The district derived its name from the name of Guru Dronacharya, the village was given as *gurudakshina* to him by his students, i.e. *Pandavas* and hence it came to be known as Guru-gram, which in course of time got distorted to Gurgaon. Thus, the district has been in existence since the times of Mahabharata. The district is surrounded by Delhi and Rajasthan.[32]

Gurgaon is the southern-most district of Haryana. On its north, it is bounded by the district of Rohtak and the union territory of Delhi. Faridabad district lies to its east. On its south, the district shares boundaries with the states of Uttar Pradesh and Rajasthan in the south, to its west lies the district of Rewari and the state of Rajasthan.

The district has an area of 2766 sq. km. It comprises of three Sub-divisions, seven Tahsils, two Sub-Tahsils and nine blocks as shown in Table 1.14.

The total population of Gurgaon is 16,57,669. The literate population is 8,45,103 out of which 5,45,481 are males and 2,99,622 are females. The sex ratio is 874. Density of population is 598.[33]

TABLE 1.14

Administrative Structure of Gurgaon District

Sub-divisions	*Tahsils*	*Sub-Tahsils*	*Blocks*
(1) Gurgaon	(1) Gurgaon	(1) Nagina	(1) Farukh Nagar
(2) Nuh	(2) Pataudi	(2) Farukh Nagar	(2) Ferozepur Jhirka
(3) Ferozepur Jhirka	(3) Nuh		(3) Gurgaon
	(4) Ferozepur Jhirka		(4) Nagina
	(5) Punhana		(5) Nuh
	(6) Sohana		(6) Pataudi
	(7) Taoru		(7) Punhana
			(8) Sohana
			(9) Taoru

Source: Statistical Abstract of Haryana, 2000-01, p. 18.

(12) Rewari District

Rewari was accorded the status of a district by the Government of Haryana on November 1, 1989. Is geographical boundaries have district Rohtak in its north, Mahindragarh district in its west and district Gurgaon in its east and north-east directions. District Alwar of Rajasthan touches Rewari in the south-east. Prior to it, Rewari was a sub-division and Tahsil headquarter of district Mahindragarh.

The district has an area of 1582 sq. km. It comprises of two Sub-divisions, three Tahsils, one Sub-Tahsil and five Blocks as shown in the Table 1.15.

TABLE 1.15

Administrative Structure of Rewari District

Sub-divisions	*Tahsils*	*Sub-Tahsils*	*Blocks*
(1) Rewari	(1) Rewari	(1) Dharuhera	(1) Rewari
(2) Kosli	(2) Bawal		(2) Khol at Rewari
	(3) Kosli		(3) Jatusana
			(4) Bawal
			(5) Nahar

Source: Statistical Abstract of Haryana, 2000-01, p. 19.

The total population of the district according to 2001 census is 7,64,727. The literate population is 4,92,785 out of which 3,02,243 are males and 1,90,542 are females. The sex ratio is 901 and density of population is 483.[34]

(13) Mahindragarh District

The Mahindragarh town was previously known as *Kanaud* which took its name from the *Kanaudia* group of Brahmans. The Mahindragarh district was formed in 1948 by grouping different tracts of erstwhile princely states, Narnaul and Mahindragarh Tahsils from Patiala state, Dadri from Jind state and a part of Bawal nizamat from Nabha state.[35]

Mahindragarh is bounded on the north by Bhiwani and Rohtak districts, on the east by Rewari district and Alwar district of Rajasthan, on the south by Alwar, Jaipur and Sikar districts of Rajasthan and on the west by Sikar and Jhunjhunu districts of Rajasthan.

The district has an area of 1859 sq. km. It comprises of two Sub-divisions, two Tahsils, three Sub-Tahsils and five Blocks as shown in the Table 1.16.

TABLE 1.16

Administrative Structure of Mahindragarh District

Sub-divisions	*Tahsils*	*Sub-Tahsils*	*Blocks*
(1) Mahindragarh	(1) Mahindragarh	(1) Ateli	(1) Ateli Nangal
(2) Narnaul	(2) Narnaul	(2) Nangal Chaudhary	(2) Kanina
		(3) Kanina	(3) Mahindragarh
			(4) Nangal Chadhary
			(5) Narnaul

Source: Statistical Abstract of Haryana, 2000-01, p. 19.

The total population of the district is 8,12,022. The literate population is 4,82,852 out of which 3,01,430 are males and 1,81,422 are females. The sex ratio is 919 and density of population is 437.[36]

(14) Bhiwani District

Bhiwani District which lies on the south-west of Haryana state, was carved out of the district of Hisar and Mahindragarh on 22nd December 1972, with a view to hasten the process of development in this arid and sandy area.

Total area of the district is 4778 sq. km., which is 9.22% of the total area of the state. The district comprises of four Sub-divisions, six Tahsils, two Sub-Tahsils and nine Blocks as shown in Table 1.17.

TABLE 1.17

Administrative Structure of Bhiwani District

Sub-divisions	*Tahsils*	*Sub-Tahsils*	*Blocks*
(1) Bhiwani	(1) Bhiwani	(1) Badhra	(1) Badhra
(2) Dadri	(2) Bawani Khera	(2) Bondkalan	(2) Bawani Khen
(3) Loharu	(3) Tosham		(3) Bhiwani
(4) Siwani	(4) Dadri		(4) Dadu-I
	(5) Loharu		(5) Dadu-II
	(6) Siwani		(6) Lohru
			(7) Tosham
			(8) Kairu
			(9) Siwani

Source: Statistical Abstract of Haryana, 2000-01, p. 18.

The total population of district according to 2001 census is 14,24,554. The literate population is 6,39,817 out of which 4,10,150 are males and 2,29,667 are females. The sex ratio is 880 while density of population is 298.[37]

(15) Jhajjar District

Jhajjar district came into existence on July 15th 1997. It was carved out of Rohtak district with a view to hasten the process of development in this arid and semi-arid area. It is the 18th district of Haryana state.

Jhajjar district has an area of 1,834 sq. km. The district comprises of two Sub-divisions, three Tahsils, one sub-Tahsil and five Blocks. The administrative structure is shown in Table 1.18.

The total population of the district according to 2001 census is 8,87,392. The literate population is 4,16,416, out of

TABLE 1.18

Administrative Structure of Jhajjar

Sub-divisions	*Tahsils*	*Sub-Tahsils*	*Blocks*
(1) Jhajjar	(1) Jhajjar	(1) Matanhail	(1) Jhajjar
(2) Bahadurgarh	(2) Bahadurgarh		(2) Bahadurgarh
	(3) Beri		(3) Beri
			(4) Sahalwas
			(5) Matenhail

Source: Statistical Abstract of Haryana, 2000-01, p. 18.

which 2,60,679 are males while 1,55,737 are females. The sex ratio is 848 and density of population is 484.[38]

(16) Hisar District

Hisar town was inhabited by *Firozshah Tuglak* and contemporarily known as *"Hisar-E-Feroza"*, an Arabic word meaning fort. It is one of the important towns of the Haryana state and earned a good name in the field of education and industrial growth during past two decades. It gained importance in early sixties when Agriculture University was set-up as an extension of Punjab Agriculture University, Ludhiana. Ever since, the Government's positive policies have played a vital role in the economic development of the city. The industrial policy of the Government has attracted large number of entrepreneurs and has resulted into the industrialization in and around the city.[39]

The Hisar district has an area of 3,983 sq. km. The Hisar district comprises of two Sub-divisions, four Tahsils, three Sub-Tahsils and five Blocks an shown in Table 1.19.

The total population of district according to 2001 census is 15,36,417. The literate population is 8,58,255 out of which 5,45,218 are males and 3,13,037 are females respectively. The sex ratio is 866 and density of population is 386.[40]

TABLE 1.19

Administrative Structure of Hisar District

Sub-divisions	*Tahsils*	*Sub-Tahsils*	*Blocks*
(1) Hisar	(1) Hisar	(1) Uklana Mandi	(1) Adampur
(2) Hansi	(2) Adampur	(2) Barwala	(2) Barwala
	(3) Hansi	(3) Baas	(3) Baas
	(4) Narnaund		(4) Hansi
			(5) Hisar-I

Source: Statistical Abstract of Haryana, 2000-01, p. 18.

(17) Fatehabad District

The district derives its name from its head quarter's town Fatehabad. The town was founded by *Firozshah Tughlak*. He named it after his son *Fateh Khan*. The Fatehabad was carved out of Hisar district on July 15th 1997.

District Fatehabad is located in the south-western part of Haryana. It is surrounded by Punjab in the north, district Hisar in south, district Jind in east and district Sirsa in west.

The district has an area of 2520 sq. km. It comprises of three Sub-divisions, three Tahsils, three Sub-Tahsils and five Blocks as shown in the Table 1.20.

TABLE 1.20

Administrative Structure of Fatehabad District

Sub-divisions	*Tahsils*	*Sub-Tahsils*	*Blocks*
(1) Fatehabad	(1) Fatehabad	(1) Bhuna	(1) Fatehabad
(2) Tohana	(2) Tohana	(2) Bhattu Kalan	(2) Tohana
(3) Ratia	(3) Ratia	(3) Jakhal	(3) Ratia
			(4) Bhattu Kalan
			(5) Bhuna

Source: Statistical Abstract of Haryana, 2000-01, p. 20.

The total population of the district according to 2001 census is 3,94,385 out of which 2,45,658 are males and 1,48,727 are females. The sex ratio is 886 and density of population is 318.[41]

(18) Sirsa District

The name of the district is derived from its headquarter's Sirsa. It is said to be one of the oldest places of North India and its ancient name was Sairishaka, which finds mention in *Mahabharata, Panini's Ashetadhyayi* and *Divyavadan.* The derivation of name Sirsa, is also attributed to the abundance of *siris* trees in neighbourhood of Sirsa which seems quite plausible. In ancient period, Sirsa was also known as *Sirsapattan.*[42]

The district has an area of 4277 sq. km. It comprises of three Sub-divisions, four Tahsils, three Sub-Tahsils and six Blocks as shown in the Table 1.21.

TABLE 1.21

Administrative Structure of Sirsa District

Sub-divisions	*Tahsil*	*Sub-Tahsil*	*Blocks*
(1) Sirsa	(1) Sirsa	(1) Nathusari Chopta	(1) Dabwali
(2) Dabwali	(2) Dabwali	(2) Kalanwali	(2) Baragudha
(3) Ellenabad	(3) Ellenabad	(3) Ellenabad	(3) Ellenabad
	(4) Rania		(4) Rania
			(5) Sirsa
			(6) Odhan
			(7) Nathusari Chopta

Source: Statistical Abstract of Haryana, 2000-01, p. 20.

The total population of the district according to 2001 census is 11,11,012. The literate population is 5,79,212 out of which 3,54,500 are males and 2,24,712 are females. The sex ratio is 882 and density of population is 260.[43]

(19) Jind District

The district derives its name from its headquarter's town Jind that is said to be a corruption of *Jaintapuri.* It is also said that this town had been founded at the time of Mahabharta. According to an old saying the *Pandavas* built a temple in honour of *Jainti Devi* (the goddess of Victory), offered prayers for success and then launched the battle with the *Kauravas*. The town grew up around the temple and was named *Jaintapuri* (Abode of Jainti Devi) which later on came to be known as Jind.[44]

The District lies in the north of Haryana. On its east and north-east lie the districts of Panipat, Karnal and Kaithal respectively. Its boundary line on the north forms the inter-state Haryana-Punjab border with Patiala and Sangrur districts of Punjab. In the west and south-west it has a common boundary with districts Hisar and Fatehabad and in its south and south-east lies the districts of Rohtak and Sonipat respectively.

The Jind district has an area of 2,702 sq. kms. The district comprises of three Sub-divisions, four Tahsils, three Sub-Tahsils and seven blocks as shown in the Table 1.22.

TABLE 1.22

Administrative Structure of Jind District

Sub-Divisions	*Tahsils*	*Sub-Tahsils*	*Blocks*
(1) Jind	(1) Jind	(1) Alewa	(1) Jind
(2) Safidon	(2) Safidon	(2) Pillu Khera	(2) Julana
(3) Narwana	(3) Narwana	(3) Uchana	(3) Pillu Khera
	(4) Julana		(4) Safidon
			(5) Uchana Kalan
			(6) Narwana
			(7) Alewa

Source: Statistical Abstract of Haryana, 2000-01. p. 19.

The total population of the district according to 2001 census is 11,89,725. The literate population is 6,31,238 out of which 4,03,732 are males and 2,27,506 are females. The sex ratio is 853 and density of population is 440.[45]

VIII. THE SOCIAL STRUCTURE

Like the Indian society in general, religion provides, the main basis for the structure of Haryana society. In the early times, however, the society was unireligion; the people professed Hinduism. A little later, in the 5th century B.C, two reformed form of the old religion, namely, Jainism and Budhism, came to have their hold on the people. Several centuries later, in the medieval times, there came Islam, followed by Sikhism (15th century) and Christianity (18th Century).[46] At present the society divided on the basis of all the religions is given in Table 1.23.

TABLE 1.23

Population by Religion in Haryana (1991)

Religion	*Population*	*Percentage of Total Population*
Hindus	1,46,86,512	89.20
Sikhs	9,56,836	5.81
Muslim	7,63,775	4.64
Christian	15,699	0.09
Buddhists	2,058	0.02
Jain	35,296	0.22
Others	3,472	0.02
Total	1,64,63,648	100.00

Source: Statistical Abstract of Haryana, 2000-01, p. 63.

The Table shows that Hindus Constitute 89.20 percent of total population. Sikhs constitute 5.81 percent while Muslim constitutes 4.64 percent of total population. Other religions are almost non-existent in Haryana.

Thus, we can conclude that Haryana in terms of its area and population, is small state, in natural resources it is moderately placed. Except for the Yamuna there is no perennial river here. The state is not rich in mineral resources either. The soil however, is fertile, and given enough water can yield rich harvest.

Thus, Haryana region which remained disintegrated as a political or administrative unit for a century took rebirth on November 1, 1966 representing the Consummation of the long felt needs of the region. Historically, the land is of the highest religious purity and cultural significance. Its emergence as a full-fledged state brought it into its own after a period of long oblivion. Indian tradition regards the soil as matrix of creation and civilization.

Notes and References

1. Maharaj Krishan: Tarikh-ki-Zillah Rohtak, quoted in D.C. Verma, Haryana, p. 3.
2. G.C. Avasthi: Ved Dharatala quoted in D.C. Verma, Haryana, p. 11.
3. D.C. Verma: Haryana. p. 11.
4. *Ibid.*
5. *Ibid.*, p. 12.
6. *Ibid.*
7. R.K. Sharma: Technical Change, Income Distribution and Rural Poverty, p. 1.
8. *Ibid.*, p. 2.
9. D.C. Verma, Haryana, p. 1.
10. *Ibid.*
11. *Ibid.*, p. 2.
12. W.A. Lewis. The Theory of Economic Growth, Allen and Unwin, p. 52.
13. Statistical Abstract of Haryana, 2000-01, pp. 216-17.
14. *Ibid.*, p. 321.
15. *Ibid.*, p. 323.
16. *Ibid.*, p. 25.
17. Director, Public Relation, Haryana: District Ambala—An Introduction.
18. Director of Census Operation, Haryana. (Population results 2001).
19. *Ibid.*
20. *Ibid.*
21. www.haryana.nic.in
22. Director of Census Operation, Haryana (Population results—2001).
23. Director Public Relation, Haryana. District Kaithal—An Introduction.
24. Director of Census Operation, Haryana (Population results—2001).
25. *Ibid.*
26. www.haryana.in
27. Director of Census Operation, Haryana (Population results—2001).
28. *Ibid.*
29. www.haryana.nic.in
30. Director of Census Operation, Haryana (Population results—2001).
31. *Ibid.*

32. www.haryana.nic.in
33. Director of Census Operation, Haryana (Population results—2001).
34. *Ibid.*
35. Director, Public Relation Haryana. Distt. Mahindragarh—An introduction.
36. Director of Census Operation, Haryana (Population results—2001).
37. *Ibid.*
38. *Ibid.*
39. www.haryana.nic.in
40. Director of Census Operation, Haryana (Population results—2001).
41. *Ibid.*
42. www.haryana.nic.in
43. Director of Census Operation, Haryana (Population results—2001).
44. Director, Public Relation Haryana : Profile of District Jind.
45. Director of Census Operation, Haryana (Population results—2001).
46. D.C. Verma, Haryana, p. 43.

2

GROWTH OF STATE INCOME AS INDICATOR OF ECONOMIC DEVELOPMENT

National income and in terms of a state "State Income" is an important measure of economic development of the state. Infact, the economic progress and well-being of a state depends on the size and distribution of state income. In the present chapter an attempt has been made to examine the trends in state income of Haryana specifically with reference to the following objectives:

(a) To examine the movement and growth rates of state income and per capita income at current and constant prices.
(b) To find out the relative shares of different sectors in the state income.
(c) To examine the inter-state variations in the state income of various states of Indian Union.

I. TRENDS IN STATE DOMESTIC PRODUCT OF HARYANA

In order to understand the process of economic development and structural changes occurring in the Economy of Haryana, it is necessary to analyze the trends in state domestic product of Haryana during the period of last 38 years of its existence. The study of trends can be divided into following three parts:

(a) Trends in net state domestic product at current prices.
(b) Trends in net state domestic product at constant prices.
(c) Trends in distribution of net state domestic product by industry of origin.

(a) Trends in Net State Domestic Product at Current Prices

The trends in state income at current prices is shown in Table 2.1.

TABLE 2.1

Sector-wise Net Domestic Product in Haryana at Factor Cost (Current Prices)

(Rs. Crores)

Year	*Primary Sector*	*Secondary Sector*	*Tertiary Sector*	*Total*
1966-67	356.23	79.43	94.39	530.05
1980-81	1,655.46	575.37	801.12	3,031.95
1993-94	8,315.72	4,931.31	6,174.52	19,421.55
1994-95	9,617.65	6,298.69	7,219.95	23,136.29
1995-96	9,668.34	8,110.57	8,386.67	26,165.58
1996-97	12,006.86	9,021.34	10,316.83	31,345.03
1997-98	11,867.40	10,177.35	11,865.53	33,910.28
1998-99	13,408.12	11,074.55	13,805.81	38,288.40
1999-00	14,215.96	12,231.66	16,040.01	42,487.63
2000-01	14,923.70	13,488.45	19,061.63	47,473.78
2001-02	15,443.59	14,358.51	22,782.80	52,584.90
2002-03*	15,510,39	16,487.15	25,939.95	57,937.49

*Quick Estimates.

Source: Statistical Abstract of Haryana, various issues.

It follows from Table 2.1 that in 1966-67, the primary sector comprising of agricultural and animal husbandry, forestry and logging, fishing, mining and quarrying accounted for Rs. 356.23 crores of net domestic product. This value increased to Rs. 1655.46 crores in 1980-81 and went on increasing till it touched the highest level of Rs. 15,443.59 crores in 2001-02.

The secondary sector, which comprises manufacturing units (registered or unregistered), construction, electricity, gas and water supply accounted for Rs. 79.43 crores in 1966-67, which increased to Rs. 575.37 crores in 1980-81 before touching an all time high mark of Rs. 14,358.5 crores in 2001-02. Thus, the value of net domestic product in secondary sector increased manifold during the period 1966-67 to 2001-02.

The tertiary sector, which comprised of transport, storage, communication, trade, banking, insurance and other services accounted only for Rs. 94.39 crores in 1966-67. The value increased to Rs. 801.12 crores in 1980-81 and to Rs. 22782.80 crores in 2001-02. Although the absolute share of all sectors in S.D.P. has been increasing steadily, the relative shares of these sectors have been changing slightly over the years as is clear from the following Table 2.2.

TABLE 2.2

Percentage Distribution of NSDP at Factor Cost (Current Prices)

Year	*Primary Sector*	*Secondary Sector*	*Tertiary Sector*	*Total*
1966-67	67.21	14.98	17.81	100.00
1980-81	54.65	18.55	26.79	100.00
1993-94	42.79	24.22	32.94	100.00
1994-95	42.88	24.86	32.25	100.00
1995-96	39.74	26.42	33.84	100.00
1996-97	35.53	26.99	35.27	100.00
1997-98	35.00	30.00	35.00	100.00
1998-99	35.02	28.92	36.06	100.00
1999-00	31.46	28.79	37.75	100.00
2000-01	31.44	28.41	40.15	100.00
2001-02	29.37	27.30	43.33	100.00
2002-03	26.77	28.46	44.77	100.00

Source: Statistical abstract of Haryana, various issues.

Table 2.2 reveals that the relative share of primary sector to S.D.P. was almost two-third (67.21 percent) in 1966 which fell down to less than one-third (29.37 per cent) in 2001-02. On the other hand, the relative shares of secondary sector and tertiary sector to S.D.P. in 1966-67 was 14.98 per cent and 17.81 per cent respectively, which have increased to 27.30 per cent in case of secondary sector and to 43.33 per cent in case of tertiary sector in the year 2001-02. These all changes are quite natural as a result of economic development because the role of industry sector and services sector goes on increasing with the advancement of the Economy.

The trends in per capita income of Haryana is shown in Table 2.3.

TABLE 2.3

Per Capita Income (Current Prices)

(in Rupees)

Year	*Per capita Income*
1970-71	877
1980-81	2,325
1994-95	12,900
1995-96	14,244
1996-97	16,707
1997-98	17,749
1998-99	19,716
1999-00	21,551
2000-01	23,057
2001-02	24,820
2002-03*	26,632

*Quick Estimates.

Source: Statistical Abstract of Haryana.

The Table 2.3 reveals that the per capita income of Haryana has been increasing steadily over the years. The per capita income of Haryana in 1970-71 was Rs. 877 only but it rose to Rs. 23,057 in 2000-01. Though some part of the increase reflects the impact of price inflation, it is a good sign indicating upliftment of society and higher growth rate of Economy in comparison to growth of population.

(b) Trends in Net State Domestic Product at Constant Prices

The figures of state income at current prices do not give a correct picture about the growth of the Economy, for the increase in state income at current prices reflects the combined influence of two factors, viz.,

(i) Increase in the production of real goods and services, and
(ii) Rise in prices.

If the increase in state income is due to the first factor, it is an indicator of real growth because it implies that more goods and services are becoming available to the society. However, if it is due to the second factor, it represents an undue increase of state income in money terms. Consequently, state income figures need to be deflated appropriately to eliminate the effect of any change of price level during the period. State income figures at constant prices become comparable but still they conceal the population effect. To eliminate the effect of growth of population, real per capita state product or real per capita income is calculated. Whereas the growth of S.D.P. at constant prices is an index of the total productive effort on the part of the community and indicates the rate of growth of goods and services in the Economy, the growth of real per capita is indicator of the change in the standard of living of the people. Table 2.4 reveals the state domestic product of Haryana at constant price.

The study of data in Table 2.4 reveals that the share of Primary sector in S.D.P. in absolute term was Rs. 562.73 crores in 1970-71 and Rs. 9,688.37 crores in 2001-02 while the shares of secondary and tertiary sector in absolute terms were Rs. 132.36 crores and Rs. 173.89 crores respectively in 1970-71 and the same rose to Rs. 7,633.66 crores and Rs. 12,764.74 crore respectively in 2001-02.

TABLE 2.4

Sector-wise Net State Domestic Product at Factor Cost (Constant Prices)

(Rs. in crores)

Year	*Primary Sector*	*Secondary Sector*	*Tertiary Sector*	*Total*
1970-71	562.73	132.26	173.89	868.88
1980-81	548.57	155.03	198.39	901.99
1993-94	8,315.72	4,931.31	6,174.52	19,421.55
1994-95	8,939.84	5,400.02	6,495.34	20,835.20
1995-96	8,492.59	5,786.27	6,975.05	21,253.91
1996-97	9,491.49	6,040.99	8,226.24	23,758.72
1997-98	8,615.71	6,410.22	8,940.35	23,965.98
1998-99	8,953.45	6,827.26	9,470.52	25,251.23
1999-00	9,406.41	7,118.39	10,503.42	27,028.22
2000-01	9,560.31	7,422.16	11,672.75	28,655.22
2001-02	9,688.37	7,663.66	12,764.74	30,116.77
2002-03	9,531.89	8,236.50	14,335.63	32,104.02

*Quick Estimates.

Note: The state income upto 1980-81 is calculated at 1971 prices while new series with base year 1991 was introduced in 1991.

Source: Statistical Abstract of Haryana, various issues.

The trends in per capita income at constant prices are shown in Table 2.5.

Table 2.5 reveals that the per capita income at constant price was only Rs. 877 in 1970-71 but it rose to Rs. 13,759 in 2000-01, thus registering a rise of about 1,465 per cent during the period of 30 years. It is a clear-cut indication of economic development and social upliftment of the state assuming proper distribution of increase in state income.

(c) Trends in Distribution of Net State Domestic Product by Industry of Origin

Table 2.6 provides a breakup of S.D.P. by industry of origin.

Table reveals following broad trends in changing composition of domestic product:

TABLE 2.5

Per Capita Income in Haryana State (at Constant Prices 1980-81)

(Rupees)

Year	*Per Capita Income*
1970-71	877
1980-81	1,058
1994-95	11,617
1995-96	11,570
1996-97	12,664
1997-98	12,544
1998-99	13,003
1999-00	13,709
2000-01	13,759
2001-02	14,250
2002-03*	14,757

*Quick Estimates.

Source: Statistical Abstract of Haryana.

(i) The share of primary sector which includes agriculture, mining, forestry and fishing has gone down from 64.76 per cent in 1970-71 to only 32.17 per cent in 2001-02. As agriculture contributes the bulk share, i.e. over 93 per cent to the primary sector, it would be of interest to estimate the trend of contribution of constituents of primary sector. The contribution of agriculture and animal husbandry remained between 90 to 96 per cent during the entire period while the share of forestry and mining, etc. in S.D.P. remained between 3 to 5 per cent. This only underlines the fact that in the Primary sector agriculture alone is most important and the trend and change in agriculture output determines the share of primary sector in S.D.P.

TABLE 2.6

Percentage Distribution of Net State Domestic Product by Industry of Origin

(Constant Prices)

Activities	*1970-71*	*1980-81*	*1994-95*	*2000-01*	*2001-02*	*2002-03*
Agriculture & Animal Husbandry	64.42	51.64	42.33	32.72	31.42	28.90
Forestry & Logging	0.18	0.21	0.24	0.17	0.18	0.17
Fishing	0.03	0.05	0.13	0.12	0.13	0.13
Mining and quarrying	0.13	0.35	0.19	0.34	0.44	0.20
Sub-total (Primary Sector)	**64.76**	**52.25**	**42.90**	**33.36**	**32.17**	**29.40**
Manufacturing:	9.88	13.61	18.99	19.65	18.78	20.86
(a) Registered	6.73	9.92	12.69	13.30	12.34	14.83
(b) Unregistered	3.15	3.68	6.29	6.35	6.44	6.02
Electricity, Gas & Water Supply	4.19	4.20	0.65	0.57	0.58	0.72
Construction	1.15	1.89	7.58	6.82	7.27	6.44
Sub-total (Secondary Sector)	**15.22**	**19.62**	**25.91**	**25.90**	**25.44**	**28.02**
Trade, Hotel & Restaurants	7.32	12.48	12.60	17.94	18.71	18.38
Transport, Storage & Communication	3.34	4.66	5.92	8.24	8.97	9.87
Banking and Insurance	1.07	2.05	2.76	4.50	4.90	4.16
Real estate, ownership of dwellings, legal and business services	1.74	1.92	2.81	2.48	2.40	3.05
Public Administration	2.25	2.95	2.30	2.58	2.74	2.57
Other Services	4.30	4.07	4.77	4.97	4.64	4.55
Sub-total (Tertiary Sector)	**20.02**	**28.13**	**31.17**	**40.73**	**42.38**	**42.58**

*Quick Estimates.

Source: Statistical abstract of Haryana, 2002-03, p. 199.

(ii) The share of secondary sector which includes manufacturing industries; construction; electricity, gas and water supply has shown a steady increase from 15.22 per cent in 1970-71 to 25.44 per cent in 2001-02. The major components of secondary sector are manufacturing industries and construction. The share of manufacturing in S.D.P.

increased from 9.88 per cent in 1970-71 to 18.78 per cent in 2001-02. It may also be noticed that manufacturing industries are grouped under registered and unregistered units and in both these sub-groups relative share has doubled during the period of 30 years, i.e. between 1970-71 and 2000-01. The share of registered manufacturing units increased from 6.73 per cent in 1970-71 to 12.34 per cent in 2001-02 and similarly the share of unregistered manufacturing units also increased from 3.15 per cent in 1970-71 to 6.44 per cent in 2001-02. However, the share of construction rose significantly from merely 1.15 per cent in 1970-71 to 7.27 per cent in 2001-02. The share of electricity, gas and water supply has decreased from 4.19 per cent in 1970-71 to (-) 0.58 in 2001-02.

(iii) The share of the tertiary sector which includes trade; transport, storage, communication, banking and insurance, real estate, public administration and other services increased from 20.02 per cent in 1970-71 to 42.38 per cent in 2001-02. In tertiary sector following trends are noted.

- The share of transport, storage and communication in S.D.P. improved from 3.34 per cent in 1970-71 to 8.97 per cent in 2001-02.
- The share of Banking and insurance improved from 1.07 per cent in 1970-71 to 4.90 per cent in 2001-02.
- The share of real estate, ownership of dwellings and business services improved from 1.74 per cent in 1970-71 to 2.40 per cent in 2001-02.
- The share of trade, hotels and restaurants almost doubled during the period. It was 7.32 per cent in 1970-71 and 18.71 per cent in 2001-02.
- The share of other services was 4.30 per cent in 1970-71, it rose to 4.64 per cent in 2001-02.

The structural change in the composition of state income by industrial origin is the consequence of the process of economic growth initiated during these years. Since the growth process involved a rapid expansion of manufacturing activities in the organised sector, the share of secondary sector was bound to indicate a relatively sharp increase. Similarly with the development of the Economy the share of tertiary sector was bound to increase. This development was bound to reduce the relative share of primary sector.

The theory of economic growth supports the structural change in the composition of S.D.P. The distribution of domestic product in developed countries indicates a much higher share of the secondary and tertiary sector and a lower share for primary sector. It is because of the fact that as industrialization spreads, it brings about an improvement in the share of industry and services. The Economy of Haryana is passing through this process of transition from an agricultural Economy to an industrialized one. In this process, the structural change in composition of S.D.P. is inevitable, although the structural change is taking place at a slow pace. The main reason for the slow rate of structural change in S.D.P. is slow rate of growth of secondary sector which is about 6.96 per cent on an average during the period of 32 years (1970-71 to 2001-02).[1]

As is expected during the process of growth Haryana also experienced an improvement in the share of tertiary sector. This was largely due to an expansion of transport and communication, banking and insurance and other services. The rate of growth of tertiary sector is between 7 to 9 per cent on the average which is higher than the overall rate of growth of S.D.P., i.e. 5.78 per cent.[2]

The changing structure of state income need to be further strengthened by stepping up the programme of industrialization. This does not imply a neglect of agriculture, but for accelerating the growth process in agriculture, industrialization of the Economy with the emphasis on agro-based industries and industries supplying inputs to agriculture is a necessity. It is only then that the process of transition of Haryana Economy from an underdeveloped to a developed one may be accomplished.

II. ANNUAL GROWTH RATES OF S.D.P.

Table 2.7 shows annual growth rates of S.D.P. at constant prices.

Following inferences can be drawn from Table 2.7:

- The growth rate in Primary sector is the lowest and unpredictable. It was 7 per cent in the year 1994-95 while in 2001-02 it was just 0.8 per cent, whereas for India as a whole the growth rate in primary sector in the year 2001-02 is just 5.2 per cent.
- The growth rate in secondary sector is on an average between 5 to 7 per cent whereas for India as a whole it is around 6 to 8 per cent. The

TABLE 2.7

Percentage Change in S.D.P. over the Previous Year (1993-94 Prices)

Sector	*1994-95*	*1997-98*	*1998-99*	*1999-00*	*2000-01*	*2001-02*	*2002-03**
Haryana State							
(i) Primary	7.0	-7.8	4.0	5.0	3.1	0.8	(-)0.8
(ii) Secondary	9.1	6.4	7.1	5.1	5.8	5.0	5.8
(iii) Transport, comm. and trade	5.8	7.3	3.8	14.1	16.5	10.5	11.6
(iv) Finance & real estate	6.6	13.1	1.9	8.3	0.4	8.2	5.9
(v) Community & Personal Services	3.4	5.9	16.4	3.0	0.5	3.5	3.8
Total S.D.P.	**7.1**	**1.4**	**5.6**	**7.0**	**6.4**	**5.1**	**5.2**
India							
(i) Primary	5.3	-1.5	6.6	1.4	-0.2	5.2	—
(ii) Secondary	10.3	3.8	3.6	5.2	-7.0	3.5	—
(iii) Transport, comm. and trade	10.4	7.7	7.1	7.6	6.9	8.7	—
(iv) Finance & real estate	5.6	11.6	8.4	10.6	3.5	4.5	—
(v) Community & Personal Services	3.2	11.7	9.9	11.6	5.6	5.6	—
Total G.D.P.	**7.3**	**4.8**	**6.6**	**6.1**	**4.4**	**5.6**	—

*Quick Estimates.

Source: Statistical Abstract of Haryana, 2001-02, p. 206.

growth rate of secondary sector in 2001-02 for Haryana is 5.0 per cent whereas for India as a whole it is 3.5 per cent.

- The growth rate of transport communication is 16.5 per cent in 2001-02 whereas for India it is 8.7 per cent.
- The growth rate of finance and real estate for Haryana is 8.2 per cent in 2001-02 whereas it is 4.5 per cent for India.
- Community and personal services grew at the rate of 3.5 per cent in Haryana in 2001-02 whereas the growth rate for India as a whole is 5.6 per cent.

The Table indicates that growth of S.D.P. in Haryana is on an average between 5 to 7 per cent. The growth rate is highest in tertiary sector followed by secondary and primary sector respectively.

III. INDICES OF STATE DOMESTIC PRODUCT

The indices of S.D.P. also reveals that the components of tertiary and secondary sector have registered a rapid growth than the components of primary sector. The Table 2.8 shows the indices of S.D.P. at constant price.

The Table shows that components of tertiary and secondary sector are experiencing a faster growth than primary sector. The Table reveals following results:

- The indices of primary sector at constant prices stood at 116.5 in 2001-02, showing an increase of 16.5 per cent over the base year 1993-94.
- The indices of secondary sector at constant prices increased to 155.4 in 2001-02, showing an increase of 55.4 per cent over the base year 1993-94.
- The indices of Transport and communication at constant prices was 228.1 in 2001-02 showing an increase of 128.1 per cent over the base year 1993-94.
- The indices of finance and real estate showed an increase of 102.8 per cent in 2001-02 over the base

TABLE 2.8

Indices of Net State Domestic Product at Factor Cost by Major Sources in Haryana (1993-94 = 100)

Particular	*1993-94*	*1997-98*	*1998-99*	*1999-00*	*2000-01*	*2001-02*	*2002-03*
N.S.D.P. (Index)							
(i) At Current Prices	100.0	174.6	197.1	218.8	244.4	270.8	298.3
(ii) At 1993-94 Prices	100.0	123.4	130.0	139.9	147.5	155.1	165.3
(a) Primary Sector							
(i) At Current Prices	100.0	142.7	161.2	171.0	179.5	185.7	186.5
(ii) At 1993-94 Prices	100.0	103.6	107.7	113.1	115.0	116.5	114.6
(b) Secondary Sector							
(i) At Current Prices	100.0	206.4	224.6	248.0	273.5	291.2	334.3
(ii) At 1993-94 Prices	100.0	130.0	138.8	144.4	150.5	155.4	167.0
(c) Transport, Comm. & Trade							
(i) At Current Prices	100.0	192.6	213.4	253.8	315.6	370.0	432.5
(ii) At 1993-94 Prices	100.0	148.5	154.2	177.1	205.1	228.1	267.4
(d) Finance & Real Estate							
(i) At Current Prices	100.0	200.6	225.8	258.7	283.5	427.5	468.8
(ii) At 1993-94 Prices	100.0	160.2	161.9	176.0	184.7	202.8	205.7
(e) Community and Personal Services							
(i) At Current Prices	100.0	184.7	248.0	275.8	310.3	322.2	351.6
(ii) At 1993-94 Prices	100.0	123.8	144.8	147.9	151.3	155.3	162.3
(f) Per capita N.S.D.P.							
(i) At Current Prices	100.0	160.0	177.8	194.3	214.1	221.8	240.3
(ii) At 1993-94 Prices	100.0	113.1	117.2	123.6	129.2	127.0	133.2

Source: Statistical Abstract of Haryana, 2002-03, pp. 204-05.

year 1993-94.

- The indices of community and personal services showed an increase of 55.3 per cent in 2001-02 over the base year 1993-94.

Thus we may conclude on the basis of Table 2.8 that the Tertiary sector is experiencing maximum growth followed by secondary and primary sector respectively.

IV. INTER-STATE VARIATION IN INCOME

For computing aggregate income of respective states in India, State domestic products (SDP) of various states are estimated regularly for every year by its governments agencies. The data related to SDP estimates are widely in use by various agencies like Planning Commission, Finance Commission and other research organisations for assessing the degree of regional disparities and also for formulating necessary policies in connection with transfer of resources from centre to states. The estimates of SDP can be successfully utilized for measuring the degree of development attained by a state. Accordingly, the level of development attained by state can also be measured by its per capita income which can again be compared with the all India average of per capita income. The SDP estimate also work as useful indicators to show structural transformation, if any, among the constituent sectors of these states. The CSO estimate of per capita income of 15 major states of India is given in Table 2.9 to access the ratio of disparity between various states of Indian union.

The Table 2.9 reveals that during 21 year period, i.e. from 1980-81 to 2000-01, the per capita income figures of most of the states, excepting a few rich states like Punjab, Haryana and Maharashtra have gone for a little change. Moreover, the relative ranking of the most of states by per capita income has not shown any change excepting Himachal Pradesh, Madhya Pradesh, West Bengal and Tamil Nadu. But the poorest states in respect of per capita income during the same period were Bihar, Orissa, Assam, Uttar Pradesh, Rajasthan, Madhya Pardesh. The per capita income figure of Bihar continues to be lowest among all the 16 states.

The Table further reveals that inter-state disparity in respect of per capita income has widened during the 21 year period as a result of the strategy followed in planning for economic development in India. As a result of this, the disparity ratio between the rich poor states has widened. The disparity between Punjab and poorest state Bihar which were 2.91:1 in 1980-81 gradually increased to 3.90:1 in 2000-01. Thus, the planning process followed in India has totally

TABLE 2.9

Per Capita Income of Major States (Constant Prices)

(Fig. in Rupees)

States	*1980-81*		*2000-01*	
	Per Capita Income	*Rank*	*Per Capital Income*	*Rank*
Punjab	2,674	1	14,678	4
Maharashtra	2,422	2	15,410	3
Haryana	2,370	3	13,709	5
Gujarat	1,948	4	13,434	6
H. Pradesh	1,704	5	9,177	12
West Bengal	1,611	6	9,425	10
Karnataka	1,528	7	10,928	8
Kerala	1,510	8	9,678	9
Tamil Nadu	1,498	9	12,504	7
Andhra Pradesh	1,380	10	9,318	11
Madhya Pradesh	1,333	11	7,350	14
Uttar Pradesh	1,278	12	6,373	15
Orissa	1,231	13	5,411	17
Rajasthan	1,222	14	8,272	13
Assam	1,200	15	5,978	16
Bihar	919	16	3,768	18

Note: Estimates for 1980-81 at 1980-81 prices while estimates for 2000-01 are at 1993-94 prices.

Source: Compiled from C.S.O. estimates, Statistical Abstract of Haryana, 2000-01, p. 198.

failed in fulfilling one of its objectives of removing regional imbalances and maintaining balanced regional development throughout the country.

Economists, however prefer to use SDP estimates at current prices for the purpose of comparison. The reason for using current price estimates are as follows:

(a) The database of real income at the state level is weaker than the data base of the current price estimates. Consequently, the current price data are considered more reliable although only relatively.

(b) There is difference in methodology, source material used and base year for constant price estimates.

TABLE 2.10

Per Capita Income of Major States (Current Prices)

(in Rupees)

States	*1980-81*		*2000-01*	
	Per capita income	*Rank*	*Per capita income*	*Rank*
Delhi*	—		35,705	1
Goa*	—		24,309	2
Punjab	2,675	1	23,040	4
Maharashtra	2,427	2	23,398	3
Haryana	2,370	3	21,114	5
Gujarat	1,951	4	18,625	7
Himachal Pradesh	1,698	5	15,012	11
Jammu & Kashmir	1,649	6	12,338	14
Karnataka	1,596	7	16,343	9
West Bengal	1,564	8	15,569	10
Tamil Nadu	1,498	9	19,141	6
Kerala	1,494	10	18,262	8
Andhra Pradesh	1,380	11	14,715	12
Uttar Pradesh	1,286	12	9,765	16
Orissa	1,231	13	9,162	18
Rajasthan	1,222	14	12,533	13
Assam	1,200	15	9,612	17
Madhya Pradesh	1,183	16	10,907	15
Bihar	878	17	638	19
All India	1,630		17,039	

* Delhi and Goa were not granted the status of state in 1980-81.

Source: Complied from C.S.O. estimates. Indian Economic Survey, 2001-02, p. S-12.

Thus the estimates of S.D.P. at constant prices are not considered very reliable for comparison purposes. The comparison of S.D.P. of various states at current prices is shown in the Table 2.10.

Table 2.10 shows that in 1980-81 per capita net state domestic product of only six states, i.e. Punjab, Haryana,

Maharashtra, Gujarat, Himachal Pradesh and J & K was above the national average, whereas in 1999-2000, nine states, namely, Goa, Delhi, Punjab, Maharashtra, Haryana, Gujarat, Tamilnadu Kerala were having per capita income above the national average. The states of T.N. and Kerala have improved their relative position while Himachal Pradesh and J & K have gone below the national average. The disparity ratio between the rich state of Punjab, and poor state of Bihar which was 1: 3.04 in 1980-81 gradually increased to 1: 4.16 in 1999-2000. Thus, it proves that the planning process in India has failed to reduce regional disparities to a considerable extent. Moreover, the Table shows the relative ranking of Tamilnadu and Kerala have improved considerably. But the same ranking has deteriorated considerably for J & K, Himachal Pradesh and U.P.

Table 2.10 clearly depicts that Haryana's per capita net state domestic product has always been higher in comparison to national average. In the year 1980-81, national average was Rs. 1,630 while it was Rs. 2,370 (1.45 times) in Haryana. Similarly, these figures were Rs. 17,039 and 21,114 (1.24 times) respectively in the year 1999-2000. Another very important feature relating to Haryana is that it was occupying 4th rank in the per capita net state domestic product in the year 1980-81 which slipped to rank 5th. It indicates that Haryana's Economy is moving forward and maintaining pace with all developed states. In comparison to neighbouring states its per capita income is marginally behind Punjab but significantly higher in comparison of Himachal Pradesh. Moreover, it is 2.16 times to per capita income of U.P. In fact, all round efforts of state government has contributed to mechanisation and modernisation of agriculture, intensification of industrial activities and expansion of services sector. All these efforts have led to overall development of the state and in terms of S.D.P. it is maintaining its position among the top states of Indian Union.

Notes and References

1. Statistical Abstract of Haryana, 2001-02.
2. *Ibid.*

3

HUMAN RESOURCE DEVELOPMENT IN HARYANA

The term Human Resource means the size of population of a country alongwith its efficiency, educational qualities, productivity, organizational abilities and far sightedness. According to Leon C. Megginson the term human resource can be thought of as "the total knowledge, skills, creative abilities, talent and aptitudes of an organisation or nation workforce, as well as the value, attitudes and beliefs of the individual involved."[1] Infact, human resource means human capital and human capital implies the abilities, skills and technical know-how among the population of the country.

It is worth-mentioning that human resource must be considered from both the angles, i.e. assets as well as liabilities connected with the attainment of economic development. For the attainment of economic development, proper utilization of both—natural as well as human-resources is very much essential. In the words of Richard T. Gill, "Economic development is not a mechanical process. It is a human enterprise and like all human enterprises, its outcome will depend finally on the skill, the quality and attitude of the man who undertake it.[2] Similarly, Arthur Lewis wrote, "Growth is the result of human effort.[3] It should also be noted that economic development does not depend merely on the existence of natural resources, but proper utilization of natural endowments is necessary and it depends very much on the extent and efficiency of human resources as Curl Adam wrote, "The difference in the level of Economic Development of the countries is largely a reflection of the difference in quality of their human resource."[4] Thus, from the point of view of economic welfare, it is quite essential to study human resources, in detail. It should be equally stressed that human beings are the vital instruments of production and at the same time, fruits of all economic activities are rested on the betterment of condition of living of human beings. Thus in view of its importance, it is quite essential to know the demographic features of human resource of Haryana.

I. DEMOGRAPHIC PROFILE OF HARYANA

A demographic profile of Haryana can be prepared out of data collected by the office of the Registrar General of India who is responsible authority for conducting an all India census of population every ten years. This census of India unleashes a vast store of official data relating to the demographic scene in the country. It is with the help of this that a concise demographic profile of the Haryana has been prepared as discussed in succeeding pages.

The demographic profile of Haryana can be divided into six parts, i.e.

(a) Size and Trend of population
(b) Growth rate of population
(c) Sex Composition
(d) Density of population
(e) Sex ratio
(f) Literacy

(a) Size and Trend of Population

Haryana accounts for 2.5 per cent of the total population of India. It ranks 16th according to the size of its population among the 28 states and 7 union territories as per census 2001. Haryana's position in total population of India is shown in Table 3.1.

TABLE 3.1

Population, Percentage, Decadal Growth Rates: 1981-91 and 1991-01

Sl. No.	India/State	Total Population		Percentage decadal growth	
		1991	2001	1981-91	1991-01
	INDIA	**846,387,888**	**1,027,015,247**	**23.86**	**21.34**
1.	J & K	7,803,900	10,069,917	30.34	29.04
2.	H.P.	5,170,887	6,077,248	20.79	17.53
3.	Punjab	20,281,969	24,289,296	20.81	19.76
4.	Uttaranchal	7,113,483	8,479,562	24.23	19.20
5.	Rajasthan	44,005,990	56,473,122	28.44	28.33
6.	Haryana	16,463,648	21,082,089	27.41	28.06
7.	U.P.	131,998,804	166,052,859	25.55	25.80
8.	Bihar	64,530,554	82,878,796	23.38	28.43
9.	Sikkim	406,457	540,493	28.47	32.98
10.	Arunachal Pradesh	864,558	1,091,117	36.83	26.21
11.	Nagaland	1,209,546	1,988,636	56.08	64.41
12.	Manipur	1,837,149	2,388,634	29.29	30.02
13.	Mizoram	689,756	891,058	39.70	29.18
14.	Tripura	2,757,205	3,191,168	34.30	15.74
15.	Meghalaya	1,774,778	2,306,069	32.86	29.94
16.	Assam	22,414,322	26,638,407	24.24	18.85
17.	West Bangal	68,077,965	80,221,171	24.73	17.84
18.	Jharkhand	21,843,911	26,909,428	24.03	23.19
19.	Orissa	31,659,736	36,706,920	20.06	15.94
20.	Chhatisgarh	17,614,928	20,795,926	25.73	18.06
21.	Madhya Pradesh	48,566,242	60,385,118	27.24	24.34
22.	Gujarat	41,309,582	50,596,992	21.19	22.48
23.	Maharashtra	78,937,187	96,752,247	25.73	22.57
24.	Andhra Pradesh	66,508,008	75,727,541	24.20	13.86
25.	Karnataka	44,977,201	52,733,958	21.12	17.25
26.	Goa	1,169,793	1,343,998	16.08	14.89
27.	Kerala	29,098,518	31,838,619	14.32	9.42
28.	Tamil Nadu	55,858,946	62,110,839	15.39	11.19
29.	Pondicherry	807,785	973,829	33.64	20.54

Source: Census of India 2001.

It is evident from Table 3.1 that the growth rate of Haryana has exceeded that of Punjab (19.76%) and H.P. (17.53%) and even U.P. (25.80%). It is near to Rajasthan (28.3%) in the 2001 census. The population of various districts of Haryana has been depicted in Table 3.2.

TABLE 3.2

Ranking of Districts of Haryana by Population Size in 1991 and 2001

Rank in 2001	*District*	*Population 2001*	*%age of Total Population*	*Population 1991*	*%age of Total Population*	*Rank in 1991*
1.	Faridabad	21,93,276	10.40	14,77,240	8.97	1
2.	Gurgaon	16,53,669	7.86	11,46,090	6.96	4
3.	Hisar	15,36,417	7.29	12,09,238	7.34	2
4.	Bhiwani	14,24,554	6.76	11,63,400	7.07	3
5.	Sonipat	12,78,830	6.07	10,45,158	6.35	5
6.	Karnal	12,74,843	6.05	10,35,390	6.29	6
7.	Jind	11,89,725	5.64	9,80,434	5.96	7
8.	Sirsa	11,11,012	5.27	9,03,536	5.49	8
9.	Ambala	10,13,660	4.81	8,06,482	4.90	9
10.	Yamuna Nagar	9,82,369	4.66	8,06,279	4.90	10
11.	Panipat	9,67,338	4.59	6,98,103	4.24	14
12.	Kaithal	9,45,631	4.48	7,81,814	4.75	11
13.	Rohtak	9,40,036	4.46	7,76,966	4.72	12
14.	Jhajjar	8,87,392	4.21	7,15,136	4.34	13
15.	Kurukshetra	8,28,120	3.93	6,69,346	4.07	16
16.	Mahindragarh	8,12,022	3.85	6,81,869	4.14	15
17.	Fatehabad	8,06,158	3.82	6,46,160	3.92	17
18.	Rewari	7,64,727	3.63	6,10,611	3.71	18
19.	Panchkula	4,69,210	2.22	3,10,396	1.88	19

Source: Census Department, Haryana (Statistical Abstract of Haryana, 2000-01, p. 39).

Table 3.2 shows that Faridabad district occupies the 1st place in the state by recording the highest population of 21,93,276 in 2001 census. It occupies the first position (with 10.4% population of the state) and has witnessed 48.47%

growth rate during the last decade caused by industrial development attracting in-migrants. The newly created district of Panchkula is the least populated district with a population of 4,69,210. The districts are arranged in descending order of their size of population in this Table 3.2.[5]

As per present jurisdiction, Gurgaon district whose rank was 4th according to size of population in 1991 has elevated its position to 2nd with 7.36% of the states total population in 2001 because of industrial development and being nearer to Delhi, the national capital of India, attracting in-migration of not only of industrial workers but also of public at large for whom comparatively cheaper accommodation and less polluted atmosphere is available. It will be seen from Table 3.2 that there are nine districts whose individual population has been counted more than 10 lakhs, namely, Faridabad, Gurgaon, Hisar, Bhiwani, Sonipat, Karnal, Jind, Sirsa and Ambala. The population of the remaining ten districts is less than 10 lakhs each.

(b) Growth Rate of Population

It is a matter of concern that at the national level the population growth has declined whereas the percentage decadal growth rate of Haryana has risen slightly from 27.41 (1981-91) to 28.06 (1991-2001). The decadal growth rate for India as a whole has been worked out to 21.34 per cent during 1991-2001 as against 23.86 per cent in 1981-91. The average annual exponential growth rate for India as a whole declined from 2.14 in 1981-91 to 1.93 in 1991-2000, while for Haryana it has increased from 2.42 in 1981-91 to 2.47 in 1991-2001[6] which is cause of worry for planners in Haryana.

The Table 3.3 shows percentage decadal variation in population since 1961.

The decadal percentage variation of the area now known as Haryana was (-) 9.70 during 1901-11, +1.95 during 1911-21, +7.60 during 1921-31, +15.63 during 1931-41, and +7.60 during 1941-51. The comparatively low growth rate of population during 1941-51 was attributed to the partition of the country by which Muslim population out-migrated to Pakistan.[7] The percentage decadal growth was +33.79 during 1951-61, +32.22 during 1961-71, +28.75 during 1971-81, 27.41

TABLE 3.3

Percentage Decadal Variation in Population Since 1961 for State and Districts

Sr. No.	*State/District*	*1961-71*	*1971-81*	*1981-91*	*1991-01*
	HARYANA	**32.22**	**28.75**	**27.40**	**28.06**
1.	Panchkula	33.54	40.08	57.61	51.16
2.	Ambala	18.90	22.11	22.31	25.69
3.	Yamuna Nagar	29.24	32.26	27.41	21.84
4.	Kurukshetra	36.07	16.59	23.40	23.72
5.	Kaithal	37.96	39.98	20.90	20.95
6.	Karnal	30.50	33.96	24.76	23.13
7.	Panipat	28.24	32.61	37.65	38.57
8.	Sonipat	24.31	23.46	24.53	22.36
9.	Jind	36.16	25.21	23.03	21.35
10.	Fatehabad	49.83	32.07	26.08	24.76
11.	Sirsa	43.96	32.51	27.79	22.96
12.	Hisar	33.98	27.32	22.67	27.06
13.	Bhiwani	30.38	30.72	22.80	22.45
14.	Rohtak	26.02	20.84	17.79	20.99
15.	Jhajjar	27.79	22.89	21.37	24.09
16.	Mahindragarh	24.62	25.79	27.91	19.09
17.	Rewari	24.00	24.52	25.62	25.24
18.	Gurgaon	34.03	29.16	32.67	44.64
19.	Faridabad	49.19	40.27	49.81	48.47

Source: Census Department, Haryana (Population results, 2001, p. 42).

during 1981-91 and 28.06 during 1991-2001. The relatively low growth rate during 1971-81 and thereafter may be attributed to the impact of family welfare schemes in the state and alertness of the people in limiting their families with the spread of education.

There are only four districts that witnessed comparatively higher decadal growth rate than the state average (28.06 per cent) during 1991-2001 and these are Panchkula (51.16), Faridabad (48.47), Gurgaon (44.64) and Panipat (38.57). The decadal growth rate is as low as 19.09

per cent in Mahindragarh district. It can also be seen from Table 3.3 that since the formation of Haryana population growth rate has remained high persistently in Panchkula, Faridabad, Hisar, Ambala and Rewari. It has been low and declining in Kurukshetra, Karnal, Sonipat, Jind, Fatehabad, Sirsa, Bhiwani and Mahindragarh. It indicates future regional imbalances in the state, which needs careful attention of policy planners and cannot be left to chance.

(c) Density of Population

The density of population conveys land-man ratio and is normally calculated as number of persons per sq. km. The density of population of a country or a state does not establish any indisputable relationship with level of economic development. Density of population that can be supported in any country or state depends upon the availability of natural resources, climate, topography and the extent of the use of technology to exploit the resource. In other words, natural resources coupled with the degree of industrialization determines the extent to which a higher density of population can be supported. For instance, Faridabad district in Haryana supports a higher density (1020 per sq. km.). The main reason for this is that Faridabad has industrialized itself whereas the districts like Sirsa, Bhiwani have low density due to being predominantly agricultural in case of Sirsa, lack of irrigational facilities and climate in case of Bhiwani.

The density of population in Haryana has thus increased from 128 in 1951 to 372 persons per square kilometer in 1991 and to 477 persons per square kilometers in 2001. The density of population in various districts of Haryana is shown in Table 3.4.

It is clear from Table 3.4 that Faridabad district retains its position of 1991 as most densely populated district of the state. It has a density of 1020 persons per square kilometer as per results of 2001 census while Sirsa district has the lowest density of 260 persons per square kilometer. There are only three districts in Haryana, namely, Fatehabad, Bhiwani and Sirsa where density is below the national average (324 persons per square kilometer).

The density is more than 600 persons per square

TABLE 3.4

Ranking of Districts by Population Density

Rank in 2001	Districts	Population Density 2001	Population Density 1991	Rank in 1991
1.	Faridabad	1020	687	1
2.	Panipat	763	551	2
3.	Ambala	644	512	3
4.	Sonipat	603	493	4
5.	Gurgaon	598	414	8
6.	Yamuna Nagar	556	456	5
7.	Kurukshetra	541	437	7
8.	Rohtak	539	445	6
9.	Panchkula	523	436	14
10.	Karnal	506	441	9
11.	Jhajjar	484	390	10
12.	Rewari	483	386	11
13.	Jind	440	363	13
14.	Mahindragarh	437	367	12
15.	Kaithal	408	337	15
16.	Hisar	386	304	16
17.	Fatehabad	318	255	17
18.	Bhiwani	298	243	18
19.	Sirsa	260	211	19

Source: Census Department, Haryana (Population results, 2001), Statistical Abstract of Haryana, 2000-01, p. 740.

kilometer in the districts of Faridabad, Panipat, Ambala and Sonipat while it ranges between 451 and 600 in eight districts, namely, Gurgaon, Yamuna Nagar, Kurukshetra, Rohtak, Panchkula, Karnal, Jhajjar and Rewari. It is below 451 in the remaining seven districts. It reflects that regional variation in density of population in Haryana is influenced by various factors such as productivity of soils, climate, topography, industrial development, urbanization, irrigational facilities and other factors of the economic development of the area and is also associated with religious and historical importance of the region. It will be interesting to compare population and density of population of Haryana and its neighbouring states. A comparison is shown in Table 3.5.

TABLE 3.5

Population and Density of Population of Haryana and Neighbouring States

India/States	*Population*	*Density per Sq. Km.*	
		2001	*1991*
India	10,270,15,247	324	264
Haryana	2,10,82,989	477	372
Punjab	2,42,89,296	482	403
H.P.	60,77,248	109	93
J & K	1,00,69,917	99	77
Chandigarh	9,00,914	7,903	5632
Delhi	1,37,82,976	9,294	6,352

Source: Department of Census Operation, Haryana (Population Results, 2001), p. 36.

Table 3.5 shows that according to census 2001, the density of population for country as a whole is 324, whereas in Haryana it is 477. Amongst the neighbours of Haryana the density of population in Punjab is 482 while in H.P. and J & K it is 109 and 99 respectively. The low density of population in H.P. and J & K is due to inhospitable hilly terrain. The density of population in Delhi and Chandigarh is 9,294 and 7,903 respectively. The high density of population in Delhi and Chandigarh is due to high degree of urbanisation in them.

(d) Sex Ratio

In any discussion on population an inquiry into the proportion of man to woman is always an essential and relevant one. We no longer argue whether one sex is superior to the other. But are the males and females equal in number? If men are in excess, some will not get partners and in certain societies the 'bride price' will go up. Truly speaking, the equality in number of males and females in all countries and at all time is an ideal seldom attained. The imbalance in the number of males and females begins in the beginning. It is now a well-established law of nature that the male, exceed females at the time of birth. It is believed that generally 943-955 female births take place for every 1000 male births, which in effect would mean that there is a deficiency of about 50 females per 1000 males in every birth cohort. Many demographers believe that left on its own, this is an unalterable constant.

As per results of census of India 2001, there are 861 females per 1000 males in Haryana as compared to 933 females per 1000 males for India. The sex ratio in Haryana was 865 in 1991. It is clear that Haryana is a region with deficiency of females. It is surprising that sex ratio in all the districts of Haryana is below the national average (933). The sex ratio in Haryana as per 2001 census is 861. It was 868 in 1961, 867 in 1971, 870 in 1981 and 865 in 1991.[8] It is notable that the sex ratio of Haryana has declined continuously since 1981 and is at its lowest since independence.

In fact, there has been a fall in sex ratio by four points from 865 in 1991 to 861 in 2001. The declining trend in sex ratio over the years is disturbing for the planners. Studies made so far have offered several explanations for this phenomenon in the past. Some of them are a preference for male children resulting in neglect of female babies causing higher mortality rates among females, the neglect of females at all ages right from birth to death may be responsible for high mortality rates among females, etc. but of all these following causes are note worthy:

(a) Neglect of girl child resulting in their higher mortality at younger ages.
(b) High maternal mortality.
(c) Sex selective female abortions.
(d) Female infanticide.

Dr. Amitabh Kundu and Mahesh K. Sahu[9] have given five reasons for decline in Sex Ratio.

(a) Progressive under count of women compared to men in different census.

(b) An increased discrimination of females (including infanticide) in providing the minimum nutrition, access to health and other amenities.
(c) Increase in the proportion of male selective migrants from other countries.
(d) Reduction in foetal wastage, resulting in a decline in female-male ratio at birth.
(e) Female selective termination of pregnancy.

The Table 3.6 shows sex ratio for the state of Haryana and its various districts.

TABLE 3.6

Sex Ratio for State and Districts

Sr. No.	*State/Districts*	*Sex Ratio (No. of Females per 1000 Males)*				
		1961	*1971*	*1981*	*1991*	*2001*
	HARYANA	**868**	**867**	**870**	**865**	**861**
1.	Panchkula	805	819	833	839	823
2.	Ambala	828	882	902	903	869
3.	Yamuna Nagar	836	848	855	883	863
4.	Kurukshetra	853	859	872	879	866
5.	Kaithal	837	843	848	853	854
6.	Karnal	853	856	856	864	864
7.	Panipat	857	852	849	852	830
8.	Sonipat	886	866	866	840	839
9.	Jind	857	860	856	838	853
10.	Faridabad	852	870	881	877	886
11.	Sirsa	845	865	877	885	882
12.	Hisar	866	859	859	853	852
13.	Bhiwani	880	878	897	878	880
14.	Rohtak	885	878	869	849	847
15.	Jhajjar	902	903	891	864	848
16.	Mahindragarh	961	910	939	910	919
17.	Rewari	926	927	926	927	901
18.	Gurgaon	891	886	880	871	874
19.	Fatehabad	848	810	811	828	839

Source: Census Department, Haryana (Population Results, 2001, p. 42).

The Table shows that sex ratio is above the state average in ten districts. Namely, Mahindragarh (919), Rewari (901), Fatehabad (886), Sirsa (882), Bhiwani (880), Gurgaon (874), Ambala (869), Kurukshetra (866), Karnal (864) and Yamuna Nagar (863). The sex ratio is below the state average in the remaining nine districts.

(e) Child Sex Ratio in the Age Group 0-6

The sex ratio in the 0-6 age group attempts to bring out the recent changes in the society in its attitude and outlook towards the girl child. The abysmally low sex ratio in 0-6 age group shows that while the son preference has remained as before or perhaps gone up in the society, the availability of sex selective technology has led to elimination of the female child. It is also vital that the sex ratio at birth at the various hospitals and institutions is checked up. The percentage of institutional deliveries as per NFHS-2[10] are 22.3% in Haryana, these are 28.9% in H.P., 35.6% in J & K and 37.5% in Punjab. Despite having created health infrastructure for over 50 years the percentage of non-institutional deliveries being so high is not a matter of accident. With 78% of deliveries being non-institutional, it is quite likely that male deliveries are being ensured at hospitals/nursing homes and other deliveries are taking place at home. There are unconfirmed reports that in case of birth of female foetus the trained Birth Attendant/Dai simply puts a lump of salt in the mouth of the foetus and pronounces a stillborn delivery within minutes.

A study by Dr. Usha Nayar[11] states the main cause of female foeticide to be:

(i) Extremely high dowry and wedding expenses.
(ii) Poor law and order situation where parents feel unsafe about girl children.
(iii) Likelihood of daughter being killed or maltreated for dowry.
(iv) Generally low respect and maltreatment of women making mothers switch off to female child, which may suffer similar humiliation in life.

District-wise sex ratio of child population in the state of Haryana in the age group 0-6 is given in Table 3.7.

TABLE 3.7

District-wise Sex Ratio of Child Population in Haryana in the Age Group 0-6

Sr. No.	*State/District*	*Total*	*Rural*	*Urban*
	HARYANA	**820**	**824**	**809**
1.	Panchkula	837	845	825
2.	Ambala	784	772	812
3.	Yamuna Nagar	807	817	789
4.	Kurukshetra	770	772	762
5.	Kaithal	789	796	756
6.	Karnal	808	814	788
7.	Panipat	807	805	810
8.	Sonipat	783	788	767
9.	Jind	818	828	775
10.	Faridabad	830	835	806
11.	Sirsa	818	823	804
12.	Hisar	830	837	804
13.	Bhiwani	838	841	821
14.	Rohtak	796	802	781
15.	Jhajjar	805	806	803
16.	Mahindragarh	814	816	801
17.	Rewari	814	811	830
18.	Gurgaon	863	872	818
19.	Fatehabad	856	861	850

Source: Director of Census Operation, Haryana (Population results 2001), p. 50.

Table 3.7 shows that sex ratio in the age group 0-6 is above the state average in only six districts, namely, Gurgaon (863), Faridabad (856), Bhiwani (838), Panchkula (837), Hisar (830) and Fatehabad (830). The sex ratio is below the state average in remaining thirteen districts. One of the disturbing factor in above Table is that sex ratio in most of the urban areas is low as compared to rural areas which indicates high degree of female infanticide.

These aspects need urgent attention of the State Government and the State Government should lead a campaign against such sex selective practices, otherwise, in the long-run shortage of females in the society can be disastrous and can lead to:

(i) Perpetuation of crime against women.
(ii) General rise in crimes and worsening law and order.
(iii) Cross-cultural migration, which may cause racial tension in the long-run.

(f) Age Composition

The study of age composition is helpful in determining the proportion of labour force in total population. In our analysis we have divided the age composition into three categories, i.e. 0-14, 15-60 and 60 and above as shown in Table 3.8.

TABLE 3.8

Age Composition of Population in 1991

Age Group	*Total Population*	*Males*	*Females*	*%age of Total*
0-14	6,462,114	3,454,217	3,007,897	39.25
15-60	8,725,803	4,713,161	4,012,642	53.00
60 and above	1,275,731	660,096	615,635	7.75

Note: 2001 Data is not available.

Source: Census Department, Haryana, Published in Statistical Abstract of Haryana, 2000-01, p. 62.

The figure in Table 3.9 indicates that proportion of child population in the 0-14 age group was 39.25% in 1991. The principal reason for higher child population in Haryana is high birth rate. The recent decline in infant mortality has also added to our child population. A high proportion of children only reflect a large proportion of non-productive consumers. To reduce the percentage of non-productive consumers, it is essential to bring down the birth rate.

The proportion of population in age group 15-60 and 60 and above is 53% and 7.75% respectively. The high proportion of population in age group 15-60 indicates young profile of population of Haryana.

(g) Literacy

A number of empirical studies have demonstrated a positive relationship between education and level of economic development. To quote the World Bank "Developing Countries with high literacy rates have tended to grow faster, even after allowance are made for differences in incomes and physical investment, and they have had higher physical investment rates.[12] The improvement in literacy contribute substantially to development is borne out by the higher degree of correlation of literacy rates with other development indicators. The female literacy rate at ages 15 and over is quite positively correlated with percentage of female workers in modern occupations, age of marriage, and contraceptive use. It is strongly and negatively correlated with infant mortality and fertility. It is in this backdrop that a study literacy rate acquires significance. According to Census definition a person who can read and write with understanding in any language is taken as literate. A person who can merely read but cannot write is not counted as literate. It is not necessary that a person who is literate should have received any formal education or should have been treated as illiterate even if they are going to school and have learnt to read and write a few words. In the past, census of India treated children below 5 years of age as illiterate. Since ability to read and write with understanding is not ordinarily achieved until one had some schooling or had at least some chance to develop these skills. Therefore, it was felt by the Ministry of Human Resource Development and the Planning Commission that the population aged seven years and above should be classified as literate or illiterate. In view of this, as in 1991 census, the question on literacy was canvassed only for population aged seven years and above in 2001 census.

Strictly speaking, while working out meaningful literacy rate, one should no include the younger population, which by definition is treated as illiterates as their inclusion in the denominator distorts the rates. For effective literacy rates, 0-6 age group is excluded from total literacy.

Table 3.9 indicates the literacy rates in the state as a whole since 1971.

TABLE 3.9

Literacy Rate in Haryana

Year	*Total Literacy in%*	*Male Literate in%*	*Female Literate in%*
1971	25.71	38.90	10.32
1981	37.13	51.86	20.04
1991	55.85	69.10	40.47
2001	68.59	79.25	56.31

Source: Census Department, Haryana (Population Results, 2001, p. 41).

The above Table shows that total literacy rate was 25.71 per cent in 1971, which increased to 37.13 per cent in 1981, 55.85 per cent in 1991 and has gone upto 68.59 per cent in 2001 in Haryana.

Let us now analyse the literacy rate by sex for various districts in the state as it will help in arriving at some conclusion regarding the development of districts as far as literacy is concerned. The Table 3.10 shows the result.

Table 3.11 shows that as expected male literacy is relatively higher than female literacy rates in all the districts. Rewari district, where male literacy rate is 89.04 per cent, ranks first in the State while lowest male literacy has been recorded in Fatehabad district (68.71 per cent). Female literacy rate is the highest in Panchkula district (68.98 per cent) while it is the lowest in Fatehabad district (46.40 per cent).

The literacy rate in Haryana, both for males and females are comparatively higher than the National Average for males (75.85 per cent) and females (54.16 per cent),[13] so

TABLE 3.10

Literacy Rate by Sex for State and Districts

Sl. No.	State/Districts	Literacy Rate			
		Males		Females	
		1991	2001	1991	2001
	HARYANA	**69.10**	**79.25**	**40.47**	**56.31**
1.	Panchkula	74.15	82.74	56.17	68.98
2.	Ambala	75.54	83.01	56.78	68.49
3.	Yamuna Nagar	69.81	79.28	50.16	64.08
4.	Kurukshetra	68.92	78.23	46.56	60.76
5.	Kaithal	54.85	69.81	28.78	47.60
6.	Karnal	65.36	76.74	41.92	58.42
7.	Panipat	69.22	79.16	42.78	58.48
8.	Sonipat	75.64	83.95	45.74	61.65
9.	Jind	60.93	74.69	29.86	48.97
10.	Fatehabad	54.71	68.71	29.77	46.40
11.	Sirsa	57.21	70.93	34.02	50.31
12.	Hisar	65.01	77.62	33.41	52.09
13.	Bhiwani	70.73	81.19	35.07	53.50
14.	Rohtak	76.73	84.29	48.25	63.19
15.	Jhajjar	78.09	83.26	40.12	59.88
16.	Mahindragarh	77.17	85.31	36.75	54.61
17.	Rewari	82.31	89.04	46.34	61.25
18.	Gurgaon	67.87	77.11	34.94	48.29
19.	Faridabad	74.15	82.49	42.12	56.80

Source: Census Department, Haryana (Population Results, 2001, p. 42).

naturally Haryana recorded a relatively higher literacy rate than the National Average (65.38 per cent) during the 1991-2001. There are five districts, namely, Gurgaon, Jind, Sirsa, Kaithal and Fatehabad where literacy rate is lower than the National Average. So far as female literacy rate is concerned, it is below the National Average in seven districts, namely, Bhiwani, Hisar, Sirsa, Jind, Gurgaon, Kaithal and Fatehabad during 1991-2001.

The gap between male and female literacy has decreased fortunately in all Districts of the State (Table 3.8).

It is the least in Panchkula (13.76%) and Ambala (14.58%) and below 20% in Yamuna Nagar, Kurukshetra and Karnal Districts. It exceeds 25% in Hisar, Faridabad, Jind, Bhiwani, Gurgaon and Mahindragarh, it is maximum in Mahindragarh (30.7%) and Gurgaon (28.82%) followed by Rewari (27.79%).

The gap has fallen maximum in Mahindragarh 9.72%, Jhajjar 8.57% and Rewari 8.18% and bridged the least in Fatehabad 2.63%, Kaithal 3.86% and Sirsa (2.57%).

II. RURAL-URBAN COMPOSITION OF POPULATION

Rural and urban classification of population is an accepted demographic practice the world over. When we look at the population of different countries, we find that with development generally urbanisation follows. Some countries such as USA or Latin America consisting largely settlers, had in fact a reverse flow. People first settled in Port cities and gradually spilled over to rural areas. Such is not the case with ancient civilization such as ours. In the society like ours, the process of urbanization is rather slow, because cities fail to offer employment opportunities to people living in the countryside. Those who migrate to cities in our society are in fact pushed out of villages due to economic and social pressures; they are rarely pulled by the so-called attractions of urban life.

The study of Rural urban composition of population in Haryana is important from the point of view of Human Resource Development. Usually it is agreed that more urbanisation indicates economic development whereas an urban area is defined as one which satisfy the following requirement:

(a) A minimum population of 5000.
(b) At least 75% of male working population being engaged in non-agriculture pursuits.
(c) A density of population of at least 400 persons per square kilometer.

Table 3.11 indicates Rural/Urban composition of population in various districts of the state.

TABLE 3.11

Rural and Urban Population in Haryana (2001)

Sl. No.	District	Total Population	Rural Population	Urban Population	Percentage of Rural Population to Total Population
	HARYANA	2,10,82,989	1,49,68,850	61,14,139	71.00%
1.	Panchkula	4,69,210	2,60,538	2,08,672	55.53%
2.	Ambala	10,13,660	6,56,957	3,56,663	64.81%
3.	Yamuna Nagar	9,82,369	5,89,448	3,92,921	60.00%
4.	Kurukshetra	8,28,120	6,12,300	2,15,820	73.94%
5.	Kaithal	9,45,631	7,62,510	1,83,121	80.64%
6.	Karnal	12,74,843	9,36,211	3,38,632	73.44%
7.	Panipat	9,67,338	5,75,435	3,91,903	59.49%
8.	Sonipat	12,74,843	9,57,398	3,21,432	74.87%
9.	Jind	11,89,725	9,47,694	2,42,031	79.66%
10.	Fatehabad	8,06,158	6,64,066	1,42,092	82.37%
11.	Sirsa	11,11,012	8,18,172	2,92,840	73.64%
12.	Hisar	15,36,417	11,38,437	3,97,980	74.10%
13.	Bhiwani	14,24,554	11,54,259	2,70,295	81.03%
14.	Rohtak	9,40,036	6,10,486	3,29,550	64.94%
15.	Jhajjar	8,87,392	6,92,311	1,95,081	78.02%
16.	Mahindragarh	8,12,022	7,02,719	1,09,303	86.54%
17.	Rewari	7,64,728	6,28,422	1,36,305	82.1%
18.	Gurgaon	16,53,669	12,88,365	3,69,304	77.72%
19.	Faridabad	21,93,276	9,73,082	12,20,194	44.37%

Source: Director of Census Operations, Haryana, Statistical Abstract of Haryana, p. 42.

District-wise study reveals that ironically Gurgaon, though lying in National Capital Region (NCR) has the highest numerical strength of Rural population, viz. 12,88,365 persons followed by Bhiwani 11,54,259 persons. The third largest rural population is recorded in Hisar District (11,38,437 persons). Interestingly, Panchkula recorded lowest rural population 260,538 followed by Panipat 5,75,435 persons and Yamuna Nagar Distt., 5,89,448 persons.

In absolute terms Faridabad retained its first rank as was in 1991 census in case of urban population, i.e. 12,20,194 followed by Hisar with a population of 3,97,980. Third highest urban population was recorded in Yamuna Nagar District (3,92,921) persons, Distt. Mahindragarh recorded lowest urban population 1,09,303 persons. The second lowest urban population was recorded in Distt. Rewari (1,36,505).

Let us now analyse the contribution of various districts in the Haryana State to the rural population of the Districts. The analysis is shown in Table 3.12.

TABLE 3.12

Ranking of Districts by Rural Population

Rank During 2001 census	*State/District*	*Percentage of Rural Population to Total District Population*	*Percentage Distribution of Rural population to Total Rural Population of State*	*Rank During 1991 census*
	HARYANA	**71.00**	**100.00**	**1**
1	Mahindragarh	86.54	4.69	1
2	Fatehabad	82.37	4.44	5
3	Rewari	82.18	4.20	4
4	Bhiwani	81.03	7.71	7
5	Kaithal	80.64	5.09	3
6	Jind	79.66	6.33	6
7	Jhajjar	78.02	4.63	2
8	Gurgaon	77.72	8.61	9
9	Sonipat	74.87	6.40	8
10	Hisar	74.10	7.61	12
11	Kurukshetra	73.94	4.09	11
12	Sirsa	73.64	5.47	10
13	Karnal	73.46	6.25	13
14	Rohtak	64.94	4.08	15
15	Ambala	64.81	4.39	17
16	Yamuna Nagar	60.00	3.94	16
17	Panipat	59.50	3.84	14
18	Panchkula	55.53	1.74	18
19	Faridabad	44.37	6.50	19

Source: Director of Census Operation, Haryana (Population Results, 2001), p. 14.

The data in Table 3.12 reveals that Mahindragarh district has maximum concentration of rural population (86.54%) contributing 4.69 per cent Rural population to the State Rural Population followed by Fatehabad (82.37%) and Rewari (82.18%) having a share of 4.44 and 4.20 per cent respectively in the State's Rural population. The lowest proportion of rural population is recorded in Faridabad district which is only 44.37%, though it is making a contribution of 6.50 per cent to the State's Rural population which is more than 15 other districts of the state. The share of rural population of Panchkula district is only 1.74 in the state's rural population, which is lowest in Haryana State while Gurgaon's contribution to the rural population of the State is highest at 8.61% followed by Bhiwani and Hisar which have a 7.71% and 7.61% respective share in the State's Rural population.

It will be interesting to compare rural and urban population of Haryana with its neighbouring states and India

TABLE 3.13

Rural/Urban Population of Haryana with India and Neighbouring States

States	*Rural Population*	*Urban Population*	*Percentage of Urban Population to Total Population*
India	74,16,60,293	28,53,54,954	27.78%
Haryana	1,49,68,850	61,14,139	29.00%
Punjab	1,60,43,773	82,45,566	33.95%
Himachal Pradesh	54,82,367	5,94,881	9.79%
Uttar Pradesh	13,15,40,230	3,45,12,629	20.78%
Delhi	9,63,215	1,28,19,761	93.01%
Chandigarh	92,118	8,08,796	89.78%
Rajasthan	4,32,67,678	1,32,05,444	23.38%

Source: Director of Census Operations, Haryana (Population Results, 2001), p. 30.

as a whole. The comparison is shown in Table 3.13.

The tables shows that according to census 2001 the proportion of urban population to total population for the country as a whole is 27.78 per cent, whereas in Haryana it is 29.00%. Amongst the neighbours of Haryana, Punjab has a healthy 33.95% Urban Population while U.P. has 20.78% and Rajasthan 23.38%. The proportion of urban population is highest in Delhi, i.e. 93.01%. Chandigarh comes next with 89.78% and lowest is in Himachal Pradesh, i.e. 9.79%. This urbanisation of population is one of the index of economic development of the region.

III. POPULATION GROWTH AS RETARDING FACTOR OF ECONOMIC DEVELOPMENT

Most of the economists are of the opinion that faster population growth is a handicap in the process of economic development. In the words of Coale and Hoover "The significant feature of population is such that a higher rate of population growth implies a higher level of needed investment to achieve a given per capita output that generates a greater supply of investible resources.[14] Similarly, G.M. Meir writes, "In an under-developed country, population does not induce capital widening investment or innovation. Instead it diminishes the rate of capital accumulation, raises cost in extractive industries, increase the amount of disguised unemployment and, in a last part, simply diverts capital to maintaining children who dies after reaching the productive age. In short, resources go to the formulation of population, not capital."[15]

In Haryana, the population is growing rapidly leading to low level of income, low rate of saving and capital formation and unemployment. It would be of much interest to verify how the high rate of growth of population in Haryana is working as a retarding factor to its economic development under following headings:

1. Firstly, population has got its impact on the growth of per capita income in the state. In Haryana rising population is working as a

retarding factor in growth of per capital Income. From 1966-67 to 2000-01, S.D.P. increased from 868.88 crore to 53786.61 crore but per capital income increased from Rs. 877 to Rs. 21551[16] having low growth rate of around 2.5 per cent per annum. This is due to high growth rate of population in the state.

2. Secondly, rapidly rising population is aggravating the unemployment problem in the state creating high unemployment in the urban areas as well as huge extent of disguised unemployment in the rural areas. At the end of each five-year plan the backlog of unemployment in Haryana is increasing, as the volume of employment generated could not match the additional number of labour included in work force. The total number of unemployed persons registered with employment exchange in Haryana stood at 663775 in 2001.[17] Thus, a huge proportion of our state resources have been constantly used for generation of employment opportunities so as to clear backlog of unemployment arising from rapidly rising population.
3. Thirdly, rapidly rising population increases the number of children in the school going age and also raises the enrolment of students in college and Universities Education. All these increase the expenditure on education. Moreover, this rising population in Haryana is also increasing the burden of enhanced expenditure on medical care, public health and having accommodation.
4. Lastly, a fast growing population is reducing the state's capacity to save and invest. In a large family the burden of dependency is much higher which in turn reduces its saving capacity. Thus, the rapidly growing population reduces the capacity as well as rate of savings and investment in the state, which always goes against the strategy of development.

To summarise, it is worthwhile to quote R.H. Cassen[18] who while talking about macro-economics of population has drawn attention to two main relationships through which population growth affects economic development. These are:

(a) Saving Effect, and
(b) Composition of Investment Effect.

R.H. Cassen argues that savings are reduced by population growth because of the increase of the so-called 'burden of dependency'. With high fertility and declining mortality in younger and older age groups, the population acquires an increasing proportion of people in the non-working age groups relative to those of working age. Since all must consume while relatively fewer produce, consumption per head must rise and savings per head must fall—even if productivity is rising, savings are less than they would be with a smaller number of dependents per worker.

The Investment arguments he says that, with an increasing population a share of investible resources has to be devoted to reproducing for additional people—the unproductive facilities—particularly social overhead capital—that would be unnecessary if the population were not growing. The composition of investment is altered in an unproductive direction instead of additions to capital going to raise the productivity of existing labour force: Investment becomes merely 'demographic investment' instead of real investment.

IV. POPULATION POLICY

Haryana Government has no independent population policy and it is following population policy of Government of India. The population policy of Government of India can be studied in two parts:

(a) The National Population Policy, 1976, and
(b) The New National Population Policy, 2000.

(a) The National Population Policy, 1976

The national population policy 1976 was formulated

and announced on April 16, 1976. Prior to the declaration of this new policy, the Government's policy on population was very much confined to family planning through clinical facilities. During those time the family planning was entirely voluntary and the Government's role was very much restricted in monitoring the people to accept the family planning norms and to arrange clinical facilities and other services to those who adopted those norms. In order to induct more positive approaches in it, the new population policy was announced. The policy statement of Government made by Dr. Karan Singh, Minister of Health and Family Planning reflected these changes. The policy statement stated, "To wait for education and economic development to drop in fertility is not a practical solution. The very increase in population makes economic development slow and more difficult of achievement. The time factor is so pressing, and the population growth so formidable that we have to get out of the vicious circle through a direct assault upon this problem as a national commitment."[19]

The main features of population policy, 1976 may be summarised as follows:

(i) To raise the age of marriage to 21 for boys and 18 for girls.

(ii) To raise the monetary compensation for individual acceptance of family planning to Rs. 150 for sterilization with two living children, Rs. 100 with three children and Rs. 70 with four living children.

(iii) To introduce group incentive for the involvement of teaching and medical profession, Zila Parishad, Panchayat Samitis, Cooperative societies and also labour in the organized sector through their respective representative national organisation.

(iv) Implementation of new multi-media strategy for newspapers, radio, TV films, etc. to move from urban approach to rural-oriented approach and to spread the knowledge of family planning and family limitation.

(v) To adopt small family norms for the employees of the Union Government and necessary change to be made in their service conduct rules.

(vi) Introduction of special measures to raise the level of female education in all states.

After the announcement of this population policy, the Government took a massive drive for compulsory sterilization. The coercive methods adopted to achieve the targets of family planning discredited the entire family planning programme.

Modified Population Policy, 1977

The Government of India announced its modified national population policy in 1977. The following are some of the important features of this policy:

(i) For attaining family planning target no force is to be used. Rather the public will be motivated and induced so as to undertaken various measures of birth control.

(ii) In order to reduce the growth rate of population, the minimum age of marriage was raised to 18 years for females and 21 years for males.

(iii) In order to arouse awareness of population problem in younger generation, educational system was involved for the purpose and steps were taken to raise the level of education of female.

(iv) In order to regularize the system of marriage the registration of marriages has been made compulsory.

(v) Utilization of media so as to spread the message of family planning among the rural people.

(vi) Introducing the provision of monetary compensation to the people going for sterilization and tubectomy.

(vii) Imparting population education in the education Institution along with general education.

The modified population policy, 1977 has transformed the strategy of population control from compulsory sterilization to voluntary sterilization. Although this policy is suitable for democratic country like India but still it has resulted in stagnation in respect of family planning programme.

(b) The New National Population Policy, 2000

The new national population policy, 2000 was announced by the Central Government on February 1st, 2000. The national population policy, 2000 include the following aspects:

(i) Address the unmet needs for basic reproductive and child health services, suppliers and infrastructure.

(ii) Achieve universal immunization of children against all vaccine preventable diseases.

(iii) To promote delayed marriage for girls not earlier than 18 years and preferable after 20 years of age.

(iv) Achieve 80 per cent institutional deliveries and 100 per cent deliveries by trained persons.

(v) Achieve universal access to information/ counseling and services for fertility regularisation and contraception with a wide of choice.

(vi) Achieve 100 per cent registration of births, deaths, marriage and pregnancy.

(vii) Contain Acquired Immune Deficiency Syndrome (AIDS) and promote greater interaction between the Management of reproductive trace-infection and sex and other communicable diseases.

(viii) Integrate Indian System of Medicines in provision of reproductive and child health services and in reaching out to household.

(ix) Bring about convergence in implementation of related social sector programme, so that family welfare becomes a people centered programme.

Haryana Government is following the population policy of Government of India and to achieve population stabilization, a "State Population Commission" has been constituted. As per Guidelines of National Population Policy, the "State Family Welfare Action Plan" has also been formulated so that the programme may be implemented effectively.

The efforts of the Health Department have now started yielding desired results. The life expectancy, which was very low at the time of the freedom of the country, has now gone up to 64.64 years in case of males and 69.30 years of female. The birth rate, which was 42.1/1000 in 1971, is now 23.1/1000 as per National Health and Family Survey.[20] There is a fall in infant mortality rate also. According to National Family Survey, infant mortality rate is 56.8 per thousand in Haryana while National Figure is 67.6 per thousand.

Thus, we can say that Government of Haryana is making earnest effort to control population and improve standard of living of people. It will be only through population control the fruits of economic development will be fully realized in Haryana.

V. EFFORTS FOR HUMAN RESOURCE DEVELOPMENT IN HARYANA

In the process of economic growth, it is essential to attach more importance to the development of human resource. It is the lack of investment in Human Resource which is responsible for slow growth in many economies. The Government of Haryana is aware of the fact, and it aims to solve the problems in development of human resources by creating necessary infrastructure. The efforts of Government of Haryana in this direction can be outlined through its policies regarding education and medical facilities in the state which are discussed below:

(A) Education

The importance of education as a key to economic development has been realised only in recent times. Various studies have been conducted by economists in the west to assess the contribution of Education in economic development. Famous Economist M.P. Todarao states that education contributes to economic development in the following ways:[21]

(i) It helps in creating a more productive labour force endowing it with increased knowledge and skills.

(ii) It helps in providing widespread employment and income-earning opportunities for teachers and construction workers, etc.

(iii) It helps in creating a class of educated leaders to fill vacancies left by departing expatriates or otherwise vacant positions in government services, private businesses and professions.

(iv) It helps in providing skills and encourages modern attitudes in the diverse segments of the population.

Education is a key to development, hence education for all is one of the primary objective of Haryana state. The development of education facilities in Haryana can be studied in three parts:

(a) Educational infrastructure.
(b) Reforms in Higher Education.
(c) Technical Education.

(a) Educational Infrastructure

It has been the endeavour of the Government of Haryana to develop Educational facilities in every nook and corner of the state. There has been vast expansion of educational facilities in the state as shown in Table 3.14.

TABLE 3.14

Number of Recognised Educational Institutions in Haryana

Type of Institution	*1966-67*	*1970-71*	*1990-91*	*2000-01*	*2002-03*
Universities	1	1	3	4	4
Arts and Science Colleges	40	65	120	150	155
College for Physical Education	—	—	1	1	1
Teacher Training Colleges	5	12	18	20	21
High/Senior Secondary Schools	597	975	2,356	4,138	—
Middle/Senior Basic Schools	735	760	1399	1887	—
Primary/Junior Basic Schools	4,447	4,204	5,109	11,013	—
Teacher Training Schools	10	12	17	17	17

Source: Director of Secondary/Middle/Primary Education, Haryana, Statistical Abstract of Haryana, 2002-03, p. 121.

The Table reveals all round growth in the educational infrastructure in the state since its inception in 1967.

The Table shows that presently, there are four universities and 175 colleges functioning in the state which include 120 colleges of general education and 55 colleges are exclusively for women. The enrolment in colleges in the state stood at 1,98,585 in 2000-01, out of which, girls accounted for 43.22 per cent. The percentage of scheduled caste students in colleges was 7.35 per cent in 2000-01.[22]

The Table 3.14 shows that there are 4138 High/Senior Secondary Schools and 1887 middle senior secondary schools in the state. The number of primary schools stood at 11,013 in 2000-01.

(b) Reforms in Higher Education

Many reforms and new initiatives have been undertaken to implement the education policy in order to ensure excellence in higher education to make it forward looking, progressive and job oriented and minimizing wastage to ensure optimum utilisation of resources. Universities have introduced a number of vocational, need-based, job-oriented courses. Special emphasis is being laid by the State Government on girl's education. As a result, the number of colleges for girls in Haryana has gone upto 55. In order to promote the study of science subjects by girl students the State Government has sanctioned 380 one time scholarships to be given to girl students taking up Medical/ Non-medical group at Degree level.

Now there are at least 180 teaching days in an academic session in the colleges as against 90 to 100 days achieved earlier. Courses have been consolidated wherever necessary and obsolete courses have been weeded out while laying emphasis on new emerging areas. Efforts have been made to divert students from courses with low employability to courses having higher job potential.

Permission has been given to a large number of Aided Private Colleges in the State for starting more than 200 new courses during the last 2 years which are largely in the newly emerging areas such as Bachelor of Information Technology, Computer Application, M.Sc. Software, Master in Information

Technology, Bio-technology, Microbiology, Tourism and Travel Management, etc.

A scheme has been evolved to give recognition and encourage merit in the field of higher education. Under this scheme, meritorious students of Kurukshetra University, Kurukshetra (KUK) and Maharishi Dayanand University (MDU), Rohtak are honoured separately at State level functions. 231 students of KUK and 402 students of MDU who achieved excellence in examinations held during April, 2000 were honoured recently.

A scheme called "Earn While You Learn" has been devised and implemented in all the colleges of the State. Under this scheme, promising students who are not able to pursue higher studies for lack of financial resources have been employed by the colleges for jobs in laboratories, libraries and offices.

(c) Technical Education

The Technical Education Department provides technical manpower in the field of Engineering and Technology, Computer, Management and Pharmacy. The list of polytechnics and engineering colleges in Haryana is shown in Tables 3.15 and 3.16.

At present, there are 20 Engineering colleges, 33 other professional colleges, 26 Polytechnics and 45 Hartron workstations offering degree in Engineering, MBA, MCA, Pharmacy, Diploma and Certificate level courses with a combined intake of 21,768. Special emphasis has been laid on Information Technology (I.T.) education by providing 13791 seats exclusively for Information Technology (I.T.) related courses. Computer Engineering has been made a compulsory subject for all diploma level courses and the teaching-learning process is being carried through computers.[23]

(B) Health

Efficiency of workers depends considerably on their health. Workers whose health is not good and who fall sick quite often, cannot do their job efficiently and thus their efficiency is bound to remain low. Improvement in the health of workers automatically raises the national output. World

TABLE 3.15

Polytechnic Institutions in Haryana

Sl. No.	*Name*	*City*
1.	Government Polytechnic	Ambala City
2.	Government Polytechnic for Women	Ambala City
3.	Government Polytechnic for Women	Faridabad
4.	Government Institute of Engg. and Technology	Hisar
5.	Government Polytechnic	Jhajjar
6.	Government Polytechnic	Mandi Adampur (Hisar)
7.	Government Polytechnic	Manesar (Gurgaon)
8.	Government Polytechnic	Narnaul
9.	Government Polytechnic	Nilokheri
10.	Institute of Hotel Management	Panipat
11.	Government Polytechnic	Sirsa
12.	Government Polytechnic for Women	Sirsa
13.	Government Institute of Engineering	Sonipat
14.	Government Polytechnic	Uttawar (Faridabad)
15.	Seth Jai Parkash Polytechnic	Damla (Yamuna Nagar)
16.	B.P.S. Mahila Polytechnic	Khanpur Kalan (Sonipat)
17.	Chhotu Ram Polytechnic	Rohtak
18.	Vaish Technical Institute	Rohtak
19.	Hindu Institute of Technology	Sonipat
20.	P.D. Memorial Polytechnic	Bahadurgarh (Rohtak)
21.	Janta College of Pharmacy	Butana (Sonipat)
22.	Gandhi College of Pharmacy	Karnal
23.	Lord Shiva College of Pharmacy	Sirsa
24.	Hindu College of Pharmacy	Sonipat
25.	Dehat Vikas College of Pharmacy	Tigaon (Faridabad)
26.	Pandit B.D.S. Medical College	Rohtak

development report 1993 stated "Improved health contributes to economic growth in four ways; it reduces production losses caused by workers illness; it increases the enrolment of children in schools and makes them better able to learn, and it frees for alternative uses the resources that would otherwise have to be spent on treating illness. The economic

TABLE 3.16

Government and Non-Government Engineering Colleges in Haryana

Sl. No.	Name of the Institution	University
1.	RECK	KUK
2.	CRSEC, Murthal	MDU
3.	YMCA, Faridabad	MDU
4.	CCS, HAU, Hisar	HAU
5.	TITS, Bhiwani	MDU
6.	SJP, Radaur	KUK
7.	MM Engg. College, Mullana	KUK
8.	Vaish College of Engineering, Rohtak	MDU
9.	ITM, Gurgaon	MDU
10.	CITM, Faridabad	MDU
11.	APJ College of Engineering, Faridabad	MDU
12.	Al-Falah School of Engg. & Tech. Dhouj	MDU
13.	SKIET, Kurukshetra	KUK
14.	SBMN Engg. College, Rohtak	MDU
15.	JIET, Jind	KUK
16.	DCE, Gurgaon	MDU
17.	HCTM, Kaithal	KUK
18.	LIMT, Faridabad	MDU
19.	HEC, Jagadhri	KUK
20.	NCCE, Israna	KUK

gains are relatively greater for poor people, who are typically most handicapped by ill health and who stand to gain most from the development of under utilized natural resources.[24]

The state of Haryana has made tremendous progress in the field of health and medical services. The medical infrastructure available in the state is shown in Table 3.17.

The Table shows that health services are being provided in the State through a wide network of Government Hospitals, Community Health Centres, Primary Health Centres and various types of Dispensaries. The effort of Government is to make medical facilities available in every nook and corner of the state.

TABLE 4.17

Medical Institution in Haryana

Type of Institution	*Number*
Government Hospital	49
Community Health Centres	64
Primary Health Centre	402
District Tuberculosis Centre	12
Sub-Centres	2299
Dispensaries	29
Mobile Dispensaries	14
Dental Dispensaries	2

Source: Director Health Services, Chandigarh, Economic Survey of Haryana, 2001-02, p. 41.

The Government of Haryana has launched a number of programmes for eradication of a number of diseases. Some of the programmes are following.[25]

(a) "Pulse Polio Programme" is being launched in the State to eradicate Polio from the State. The state has already eradicated Guniea Worm Infection under the Guniea Worm Eradication Programme. The Haryana State has already achieved the target of 1/10000 leprosy cases set by the Government of India and World Health Organisation (WHO). At present, the incidence of leprosy is 0.4/10000. For this the State has been awarded a cash reward of Rs. 10.00 lakh and a citation certificate.

(b) Under the "Malaria Eradication Programme", the Health Department has done appreciable work for the control of Malaria and the incidents of Malaria have gone down to a great extent. In the year 1976 there were 7.36 lakh cases while in the year 2001, the figure came down to 1153 cases showing a decline of about 99.8 per cent. There has been no death due to Malaria since 1997.

(c) Under the "National Blindness Control Programme", Blindness Control Societies have been set-up at State and districts level to ensure optimal utilisation of Government of India funds. Against target of 1.0 lakh cataract operations, 57822 cataract operations were performed in the year 2001-02 (upto December, 2001).

(d) The State Government realises the importance of the control of Hepatitis B infection which causes various liver diseases and even liver cancer. In the year 2001-02, Hepatitis B vaccine worth of Rs. 20.00 lakh is being purchased.

(e) On the National High Way No. 1 a Trauma Centre at General Hospital, Karnal is under construction, which will be completed shortly. It is proposed to open 3 more Trauma Centres at other National Highways passing through the State, i.e. Palwal, Rewari and Sirsa. Under the Cancer Control Programme, on Cobalt Unit at Bhiwani is being set-up. The State has implemented the "Pre-Diagnostic Technique Act, 1994 since 1996." This Act has been launched to prohibit female foeticide 586. Ultrasound Clinics have so far been registered in the State out of 590. Action is being taken against faulty clinics.

(f) The State has adopted to enforce the Bio-Medical Waste Management and Handling Rules, 1998 to stop indiscriminate disposal of hospital waste. District Bio-Medical Waste Societies have been notified in all the districts and notification regarding the use of 11 Government hospitals for utilising incinerators by private hospital at a prescribed fee has been issued.

(g) "National Tuberculosis Programme" has been launched in every district of the State. Presently there are approximately 3 lakh T.B. patients in the State. To further combat the problem of T.B., revised T.B. Control Programme (DOTS) has been introduced. This programme was being introduced in 3 districts, namely, Faridabad, Gurgaon and Sonipat in the year 2000. Under this programme medicines are provided free of cost to all the T.B.

patients in these 3 districts. This programme will be extended in a phased manner to the whole of the State by the year 2004-05.

(h) The "Reproductive and Child Health Programme" has been launched in the State from the year 1997-98 for five years. The main aim of this programme is to provide quality Reproductive and Child Health Services as per the felt needs of the people. Under this project special facilities are being provided in far-flung remote rural areas.

(i) "Family Health Awareness Campaign" is being organised in the State to create awareness among masses about Sexually Transmitted Diseases (STD). As per the instructions of the Government of India, 8 Targeted Intervention projects are being run in the State under the National AIDS Control Programme. The target population for this project is truck drivers, migrant workers, commercial sex-workers, bus drivers, conductors and Jail-inmates in which they are being made aware about AIDS, HIV and condoms. The Health Department is preparing to run the School AIDS Education Programme to generate awareness among students of 9th to 12th classes in the schools. This Programme will cover 7 districts. The total number of schools to be covered in these districts is 1354. Haryana AIDS Control Society has set-up 3 voluntary counselling and testing centres at PGIMS, Rohtak, Civil Hospital, Karnal and General Hospital, Panchkula. At these centres, information and awareness on STD, HIV, AIDS and condoms is being given. Opening of such centres at Hisar, Faridabad and Gurgaon is under consideration. At present 11 STD clinics are functioning in the State for the treatment of Sexually Transmitted Diseases.

The State of Haryana has licensed Blood banks in all districts except the newly created districts of Fatehabad and Jhajjar. Presently 28 licensed Blood banks are in the State, out of which 16 are of Government, 9 in private sector, 2 in Military Hospitals and 1 of Red Cross. Professional Blood donation has been prohibited w.e.f. Ist January, 1998 and Voluntary Blood Donation is being promoted.

Conclusively, it can be said that the Human Resource Development is an emerging concept today which no country, state or organization with long-term objectives can afford to ignore or take lightly in case it wants to achieve the standards of excellence towards industrial development in particular and sustainable economic development in general. The first decade of 21st century is going to be decade of extensive changes. The proverbial element of change, namely, the political climate, the economic climate, the social climate and the industrial and technological climate are going to be far-reaching. The effectiveness of an economic system would be determined by the extent to which it can respond to these changes successfully. The changes also affect the human beings and the system has to accept the responsibility of assisting the human beings to cope with these changes themselves and also to draw up plans and design strategies for optimum utilization of available human resources in productive manner. In the present era of liberalisation and other economic reforms, development of human resources necessitates to develop professionalism among them so that they may meet the changing requirements of coming up industries and our Economy.

Notes and References

1. Megginson, Leon C.: Personnel and Human Resource Administration, Illinois, 1977, p. 4.
2. K.L. Gupta: Indian Economy (Development, Problem and Planning), 1991-92, pp. 1, 12-13.
3. Arthus Lewis: The History of Economic Growth (1965), p. ii.
4. Crul Adam: Some aspects of Educational Planning in underdeveloped areas, *Harvard Business Review*, Vol. 32.
5. Census of India, 2001.
6. *Ibid.*
7. Director of Census Operation, Haryana (Population Results, 2001).
8. *Ibid.*, p. 41.
9. Amitabh Kundu and Mahesh K. Sahu: "Variation in Sex Ratio,

Development Implication", *EPW*, XXVI, No. 41, October 12, 1991.

10. NFHS—National Family Health Survey.
11. Usha Nayar: NCERT, 1995.
12. World Bank Report, 1980, p. 37.
13. Census of India 2001.
14. Coale and Hoover: Population Growth and Economic Development in Low Income Countries (Princeton University Press, 1958).
15. G.M. Meir: Leading issues in Economic Development.
16. Statistical Abstract of Haryana, 2000-01, p. 187.
17. Economic Survey of Haryana, 2001-02, p. 74.
18. R.H. Cassen: India; Population, Economic and Society (Macmillan Delhi, 1979, p. 221).
19. Government of India: National Population Policy Statement made by Dr. Karan Singh, Ministry of Health and Family Planning (New Delhi, April 1976).
20. Economic Survey of Haryana, 2001-02, pp. 43-44.
21. Michael P. Todaro, Economic Development in the third world (New Delhi, 1987), p. 346.
22. Economic Survey of Haryana, 2001-02, pp. 46-47.
23. *Ibid.*, p. 47.
24. World Bank, World Development Report, 1993, New York, p. 17.
25. Economic Survey of Haryana, 2001-02, p. 41.

4

OCCUPATIONAL PATTERNS OF HARYANA'S POPULATION

I. OCCUPATIONAL DISTRIBUTION CONCEPT

Occupational distribution of population reflects on the degree of development and the diversification achieved in an Economy. By occupational distribution we mean the distribution of working population in various economic activities. The comparative study of working population in various economic activities is included in occupational distribution.

We generally divide the occupational activities into three sectors:

(a) Primary Sector

Primary sector includes agriculture and animal husbandry; forestry; fishing; mining and quarrying. These are called primary activities because their product is essential or vital for human existence and they are carried out with the help of nature.

(b) Secondary Sector

This includes manufacturing industries; electricity; gas and water supply; construction. This sector is called secondary as it transforms one type of input into other or raw material to finished product.

(c) Tertiary Sector

This includes transport; communication; banking and other services which help the primary and secondary activities.

The distribution of working population in these three sectors is called occupational distribution.

II. RELATION BETWEEN OCCUPATIONAL DISTRIBUTION AND ECONOMIC DEVELOPMENT

There is a close relation between occupational distribution of working population and economic development. In the initial stages of economic development highest proportion of working population is engaged in primary sector due to following reasons:

(i) In the initial stages of development in underdeveloped countries the per capita output of food products is very low. Therefore, in order to satisfy the minimum food needs, the majority of population is engaged in the production of primary products.

(ii) Most of the underdeveloped countries pay for their imports through export of primary products. Therefore, the population is engaged in the production of primary products.

(iii) The employment opportunities in non-agriculture sector remain very low.

As the economic development takes place, the production and productivity in agriculture sector, starts increasing. As a result, the working population starts shifting from agriculture to manufacturing sector as less workers are needed in agriculture than before. Another reason for increase in proportion of working population in manufacturing sector is that with the development the income of people increases whereas the demand for primary products increases in less proportion and the demand for finished product in manufacturing sector starts increasing. With the development of manufacturing sector the demand for banking, insurance, transport and other services also start increasing. As a result, the tertiary sector also starts developing, however it must be remembered here that the process of decline in working population in primary sector and increase in secondary and tertiary sector is very slow.

Famous economist Colin Clark argues that there is close relationship between development of an Economy on the one hand, and the occupational structure on the other. The economic progress, he opines is generally associated with certain distinct necessary and predictable changes in occupational structure. He writes, "A high average level of real income per head is always associated with a high proportion of the working population engaged in tertiary industries. Low real income per head is always associated with a low proportion of the working population engaged in tertiary production and a high percentage in primary production."[1] A.G.B. Fisher also reaches the same conclusion. He writes, "We may say that in every progressive Economy there has been a steady shift of employment and investment from the essential primary activities to secondary activities of all kinds and to a still greater extent into tertiary production."[2] The relation between occupational distribution and economic development can be established by analyzing historical statistical data which is shown in Table 4.1.

The study of growth pattern of developed countries reveal that higher per capita income is inversely correlated with the proportion of active population engaged in agriculture. As the development takes place the proportion of working population in primary sector declines while that of secondary sector and tertiary sector increases.

III. OCCUPATIONAL DISTRIBUTION OF POPULATION IN HARYANA

The study of occupational structure of population in Haryana can be divided into two parts:

(a) Employment aspect of occupational distribution.
(b) Output aspect of occupational distribution.

TABLE 4.1

Per Capita Income and Distribution of Labour Force in Selected Countries

Country	*Year*	*Per Capita Income in U.S. $*	*Percentage of labour force in*		
			Agriculture	*Industry*	*Services*
U.S.A.	1960	2,500	7	36	57
	1990-92	22,340	3	25	72
U.K.	1960	1,200	4	48	48
	1990-92	16,600	2	28	70
Germany	1960	1,220	14	48	38
	1990-92	20,510	3	39	58
Japan	1960	420	33	30	37
	1990-92	26,840	7	34	59

Source: United Nations Statistical Yearbook, 1977, Human Dev. Report, 1994.

(a) Employment Aspect of Occupational Distribution

The trend of occupational classification workers in Haryana since its formation has been summarised in Table 4.2.

The analysis of Table 4.2 leads to following results:

(a) Dominance of Primary Sector

It is clear from the Table that though the relative share of working population engaged in primary sector has gone down from 69.7% in 1967 to 61.7% in 1981, 58.72% in 1991 and 57.73% in 2001, there is dominance of this sector. However, if we compare it with national level, the contribution of this sector is 66.8% in 1991. Thus, it is quite favourable in Haryana in comparison to India as a whole. The cultivators constituted 48.6% of total working population in 1967. The ratio has declined to 36.47% in 2001. However, the proportion of agricultural labourers has increased from 18.1% to 20.01%. This indicates the growing numbers of landless labourers in agriculture. The percentage of workers in livestock, forestry, fishing has declined from 2.4% in 1967

TABLE 4.2

Percentage Distribution of Workers by Industrial Categories in Haryana

Sector	*% of Working Population*			
	1967	*1981*	*1991*	*2001*
Primary Sector	**69.7**	**61.70**	**58.72**	**57.73**
(a) Cultivators	48.6	44.67	38.77	36.47
(b) Agricultural Labourers	18.1	16.11	19.00	20.01
(c) Livestock forestry & fishing	2.4	0.92	0.95	1.20
(d) Mining and Quarrying	0.6	0.10	0.12	0.05
Secondary Sector	**12.1**	**15.42**	**13.18**	**14.12**
Small Scale & Large Industry	11.0	12.57	10.56	10.82
Construction	1.1	2.55	2.62	3.30
Tertiary Sector	**18.2**	**22.78**	**27.98**	**28.15**
Trade & Commerce	6.1	7.76	8.63	7.38
Transport, storage and communication	1.5	3.09	3.25	3.62
Other Services	10.6	11.93	16.10	17.15
Total	**100**	**100**	**100**	**100**

Note: 2001 Census data is not available.
Source: Census of India, 2001, statistical abstract of Haryana, 2000-01, p. 57.

to 0.95% in 1991 and 1.20% in 2001. The percentage of workers in mining and quarrying has declined from considerably 0.6% to 0.05% in 2001. However, it is mainly due to large scale mechanization in this activity. The overall picture of primary sector indicates its dominance in total working patterns in Haryana.

(b) Some Increase in Secondary Sector

In 1967, 12.1% of the total working population was engaged in secondary sector. This ratio increased to 15.42% in 1981 but gone down to 14.12% in 2001. The marginal increase in working population in secondary sector indicates that inspite of a very ambitious program of industrial development, secondary sector could not contribute much as alternative source of employment for population engaged in primary sector. However, in comparison to national level of this sector (12.7%), the position of Haryana is marginally favourable.

(c) Increasing Trend in Tertiary Sector

The proportion of working population engaged in tertiary sector has gone up from 18.2% in 1967 to 28.15% in 2001. The constituents of tertiary sector has also shown an increasing trend. The proportion of working population in trade and commerce has increased from 6.1% to 7.38% while in transport and communication it has increased from 1.5% to 3.62%. It is worth-mentioning in this sector also, Haryana is much progressive than country as a whole. The average of country as a whole was 20.5% in 2001.

The analysis of sector-wise distribution of occupational structure leads to the conclusion that despite the predominance of primary sector, there is marginal increase in the share of secondary sector and significant improvement in the share of tertiary sector which is an indication of Haryana's Economy moving towards developing status.

In order to further analyse the occupational distribution of Haryana's population let us analyse the category-wise percentage of main workers in various districts of the state. It is shown in Table 4.3.

The Table 4.3 clearly shows that Haryana's occupational structure remains primary sector-oriented, although by comparing various districts we observe that the backward districts like Mahindragarh, Bhiwani, Jind, Kaithal, etc. remain more primary sector oriented while the developed districts like Ambala, Panchkula, Yamuna Nagar, Faridabad show less orientation of primary sector. But more or less the occupational distribution of Haryana's population remains primary sector-oriented. However, it should not be taken as an indication of backwardness. In fact, it reflects the dominance of agricultural sector on the one hand and less labour-oriented industrialisation on the other. It may be mentioned that Haryana is quite progressive in agricultural sector also.

Let us now analyse the reasons in detail for the trend

TABLE 4.3

Category-wise Percentage of Main Workers to Total Workers by Districts, 2001

District	*Cultivators*	*Agricultural labourers*	*Manufacturing Industries*	*Other categories*
Ambala	16.68	13.22	3.41	66.69
Panchkula	16.70	6.07	3.07	74.15
Yamuna Nagar	17.35	15.68	3.07	63.90
Kurukshetra	23.75	22.67	1.99	51.59
Kaithal	40.47	22.55	1.67	35.30
Karnal	26.68	42.22	2.86	46.74
Panipat	23.50	14.31	4.53	57.66
Sonipat	36.42	16.73	2.16	44.69
Rohtak	39.01	12.22	2.48	46.29
Jhajjar	46.11	11.47	1.92	40.50
Faridabad	24.99	10.31	2.83	61.87
Gurgaon	31.10	9.27	2.68	56.95
Rewari	44.72	16.27	2.49	39.52
Mahindragarh	54.82	11.14	2.16	31.88
Bhiwani	52.63	11.44	2.02	33.91
Jind	50.27	16.40	1.58	31.75
Hisar	43.74	15.13	2.28	38.85
Fatehabad	44.60	22.90	2.30	30.20
Sirsa	37.63	23.88	2.18	36.31
Haryana	**36.33**	**15.32**	**2.47**	**45.98**

Source: Census Deptt. Haryana, Statistical Abstract of Haryana, 2001-02, p. 742.

of occupational distribution in Haryana which can be placed into following heads:

(a) Rapid Increase in Population

The population in Haryana has shown a rapid increase. The population is increasing @ 2% per annum. Due to this the pressure of population on land has not declined inspite of the earnest efforts of the Government of Haryana in this direction.

(b) Pre-dominance of Agricultural Sector

Despite the development of industrial sector during post-formation period, Haryana is still predominantly an agricultural Economy and therefore, majority of workers are engaged in this sector.

(c) Capital Intensive Industry

The Government of Haryana has undertaken an ambitious program of industrial development, but most of the development is in capital-intensive industry which is unable to offer new employment opportunities.

However, the development of the Economy of Haryana needs a shift in this occupational distribution and the pressure of population on land needs to be reduced. In this context, a two pronged strategy may be adopted as explained below:

Increase in Agricultural Productivity

Increased agricultural productivity is a necessity for changing the occupational pattern in Haryana. For a long time, agriculture productivity and production were inhibited by scarcity of land, fragmentation of agricultural holdings, faulty land tenure system and primitive techniques of cultivation. But since the formation of Haryana and the Green Revolution of 1968 a technological break-through in agriculture has been achieved in Haryana. The new agricultural technology consists of extensive application of artificial irrigation, fertilizers and pesticides, better and hybrid seeds, agricultural mechanization in selected promising areas. The new technology is expected to:

(a) Produce more foodgrains and agricultural raw materials needed by industries.
(b) Reduce the size of agricultural population depending on land and at the same time create fuller employment for others through multiple cropping.
(c) Help in creating alternative employment in rural areas.
(d) Generate surplus food to feed the growing non-agricultural labour in rural areas and industrial labour in urban areas.

No doubt, this agricultural strategy will reduce the pressure of population on land which will help in changing the occupational distribution in the state.

Employment Policy

A major objective of Plans in Haryana is to mobilize, to the maximum extent, the abundant labour force in the country for the purpose of economic development. Further, the productivity of labour is to be increased so that larger employment could be provided at rising levels of real income. Planned economic development is expected to lead to considerable increase in employment opportunities. Rapid progress in expanding irrigation, power, basic industries, other industries, transport and other services will generate new activities of employment. As irrigation facilities progressively increase and scope for double and multiple cropping also increases correspondingly, seasonal unemployment will naturally diminish. At the same time schemes of rural electrification will encourage the setting up of small and large workshops and factories in rural areas. Many agro-based industries will come up and provide alternative employment to agricultural labourers. Ancillary employment like reclamation work, machine repair, transport services, etc. will maintain rural employment at a very high level. In urban areas, with rapid industrialization and with corresponding expansion in transport and communication, banking and insurance and other services there would be tremendous increase in employment in the secondary and tertiary sector.

(b) Output Aspects of Occupational Distribution

According to Economists important aspect of occupational distribution is that with the economic development, the percentage of workers employed in primary sector declines while that of secondary and tertiary sectors increases. Secondly, share of primary sector in G.D.P. declines while that of secondary and tertiary sector increases. After having analysed the employment aspect of occupational distribution let us now analyse the output aspect of occupational distribution. The output aspect is shown in

TABLE 4.4

Sector-wise Net Domestic Product in Haryana at Factor Cost (Current Prices)

(Rs. Crores)

Year	*Primary Sector*	*Secondary Sector*	*Tertiary Sector*	*Total*
1966-67	356.23(67.21)	79.43(14.98)	94.39(17.81)	530.05
1980-81	1,655.46 (54.65)	575.37(18.55)	801.12(26.79)	3,031.95
1993-94	8,315.72(42.79)	4,931.31(24.27)	6,174.52(32.94)	19,421.55
1994-95	9,617.65(42.88)	6,298.69(24.86)	7,219.95(32.25)	23,136.29
1995-96	9,668.34(39.74)	8,110.57(26.42)	8,386.67(33.84)	26,165.58
1996-97	12,006.86(35.53)	9,021.34(26.99)	10,316.83(35.27)	31,345.03
1997-98	11,867.40(35.00)	10,177.35(30.00)	11,865.53(35.00)	33,910.28
1998-99	13,408.12(35.02)	11,074.55(28.92)	13,805.81(36.06)	38,288.40
1999-00	14,215.96(31.46)	12,231.66(28.79)	16,040.01(37.75)	42,487.63
2000-01	14,923.70(31.44)	13,488.45(28.41)	19,061.63(40.15)	47,473.78
2001-02	15,443.59(29.37)	14,358.51(27.30)	22,782.80(43.33)	52,584.90
2002-03	15,510.39(26.77)	16,487.15(23.46)	25,939.95(44.77)	57,937.49

Note: Figures in Parentheses are Percentages to the Total.
Source: Statistical Abstract of Haryana, various issues.

Table 4.4.

It follows from Table 4.4 that in 1966-67, the primary sector comprising of agriculture and animal husbandry, forestry and logging, fishing, mining and quarrying accounted for Rs. 356.23 crores of Net Domestic Product. This value increased to Rs. 1,655.46 crores in 1980-81 and went on increasing further till it touched the highest level of Rs. 15,443.59 crores in 2000-01. But the share of primary sector in total Net Domestic Product has a declining trend during this period. It declined from 67.21 per cent in 1966-67 to 54.65 per cent in 1980-81 and to 29.37% in 2001-02.

The secondary sector, which comprises of manufacturing units (registered or unregistered), construction, electricity, gas and water supply accounted for Rs. 79.43 crores in 1966-67, which increased to Rs. 575.37 crores in

1980-81 before touching on all time high mark of Rs. 14,358.51 crores in 2001-02. Thus, the value of Net Domestic Product in Secondary sector increased during the period from 1966-67 to 2001-02. In relative terms also, the share of the secondary sector in the total Net Domestic Product has increased over the period. It has increased from 14.98 per cent in 1966-67 to 18.55 per cent in 1980-81 and to 27.30% in 2001-02.

The Tertiary sector, which comprised of transport, storage and communication, trade, banking, insurance and other services accounted for Rs. 94.39 crores in 1966-67. This value increased to Rs. 801.12 crores in 1980-81 and to Rs. 22,787.80 crores in 2001-02. The relative share of tertiary sector in total Net Domestic Product was just 17.81 per cent in 1966-67, which increased to 26.79 per cent in 1980-81 and to 43.33 per cent in 2001-02. This means that there is an increasing trend of it over the previous years.

Thus, the sector-wise trend of growth in Haryana reveals that the share of primary sector in total Net Domestic Product is decreasing during these years. It shows the declining importance of agriculture as is expected in growing Economic due to application of Colin Clark hypothesis.

In brief we can say that:

1. There is no clear shift in the work force from primary to the secondary and tertiary sector since the formation of Haryana State.
2. The pattern of economic development since 1967 has clearly altered the relative significance of the three sectors. Primary sector which was major contributor to S.D.P. in 1967 now accord for only 29.37 per cent. Correspondingly the secondary and tertiary sectors have increased their share from 14.98 and 17.81 per cent to 27.30 and 43.33 per cent respectively. The altered pattern confirms Colin Clark's thesis that with economic development the importance of primary sector decline while that of secondary and tertiary sector increase.
3. The employment pattern of occupational

distribution has shifted towards secondary and tertiary sector but not to the extent as is desired in a developing Economy. However, it may be balanced by promoting labour-intensive cottage and agro-based industries.

Notes and References

1. Colin Clark, The Conditions of Economic Progress (1940), p. 182.
2. A.G.B. Fisher, Economic Progress and Social Security (1945), pp. 5-6.

5

EMERGING PATTERN OF AGRICULTURAL DEVELOPMENT

I. AGRICULTURE AND ECONOMIC DEVELOPMENT

Agricultural development is normally regarded as a pre-requisite of economic development. It is true that the economic development in modern times has come to be associated with industrialisation; nevertheless, it is generally accepted that industrialisation can follow only on the sound heels of agriculture, or in other words, agriculture is the foundation on which the entire superstructure of the growth of industrial and other sectors of the economy has to stand. Weak foundation would not allow a solid structure to be raised on it.

Famous economist Kuznets[1] identifies four possible types of contribution that the agricultural sector is capable of making to overall economic development. These are:

(i) Product contribution, i.e. making available food and raw materials.

(ii) Market contribution, i.e. providing the market for producer goods and consumer goods produced in non-agriculture.

(iii) Factor contribution, i.e. making available labour and capital to the non-agriculture sector.

(iv) Foreign Exchange contribution.

In short, agricultural development is the first pre-requisite for economic development.

II. PLACE OF AGRICULTURE IN THE ECONOMY OF HARYANA

The agriculture is the main stay of Economy of Haryana as about 70 per cent of total state population earn their livelihood from this sector. The agriculture is the backbone of Economy of Haryana as is clear from following facts:

(a) Share of Agriculture in the State Income

In the last 38 years of its existence agriculture has been the main source of state income. In 1970-71 agriculture contributed Rs. 559.79 crores to state income (64.42 per cent) out of total contribution of Rs. 562.73 crores (64.76 per cent) of primary sector to the state income. In the year 2000-01 the contribution of agriculture has increased to Rs. 14603.48 crores in absolute terms. Though in relative terms the contribution of agriculture has declined to 30.76 per cent,[2] it still continues to be the largest contributor to state income.

(b) Source of Livelihood

In Haryana over two-third of working population is engaged directly in agriculture. According to an estimate about 70 per cent of state population earn their livelihood from agriculture.

(c) Source of Food Supply

Agriculture is the only major source of food supply as it is providing regular supply of food to such a huge population not only of the state but also of the country. In 1966-67 the grain production in Haryana was 25.92 lakh tonnes, which increased to 132.50 lakh tonnes in 2000-01.[3] Haryana has contributed about 45 lakh tonnes to central food grain pool in the year 2000-01.

(d) Role of Agriculture in Industrial Development

Agriculture has been the major source of supply of raw materials to various important industries of the state. Cotton textiles, sugar, vanaspati, edible oil industry and agro-based cottage industries are regularly procuring their requirement of raw materials directly from agriculture.

(e) Source of Government Revenue

Agriculture is one of the major source of revenue to the state government. The government is getting a substantial income from land revenue, electricity and water bills, etc.

Thus from the foregoing analysis it is observed that agricultural development is the basic condition for the development of the Economy. *Subrata Ghatak* and *Ken Ingersent*[4] pointed out that agricultural output is very much essential for:

(i) Increasing supply of food and raw materials at non-inflationary prices.

(ii) Widening the domestic market for industrial product through higher purchasing capacities in rural sector.

(iii) Facilitating inter-sectoral transfers of capital needed for industrial development along with infra-structural development.

III. AGRICULTURE DEVELOPMENT IN HARYANA SINCE 1966

Before its formation in 1966, the Haryana territory was agriculturally a less developed part of the former Punjab. Its net irrigated area was 35.54 per cent against 58.48 per cent in Punjab. Only one in four villages was connected with metalled road. The compound annual growth rate of agriculture was in the ratio of 1:2 with Punjab.[5]

After its formation Haryana state has emerged as one of the leading states in the field of Agriculture. The main stress of economic planning in Haryana has been to increase agriculture production in the state. The agricultural development in the state can be analysed in terms of two basic components of output and input. The former represents productivity levels while the latter gives an idea of sustained development over a long period of time.

(A) Output Indicators of Agricultural Development

These indicators can be studied under two parts, i.e. Crop pattern and Yield pattern.

(a) Crop Pattern

Crop pattern represents the ratio of different crops from the point of view of the area as well as their production. Both of these are discussed below:

(i) Trends in Area under Crops

With the passage of time, there has been a substantial change in the cropping pattern of the state. With the expansion of irrigation facilities, there has been a shift in area in favour of more remunerative and less risky crops like rice, wheat, cotton, rapeseed and mustard and it has resulted into a decline in area under *bajra, jawar, maize, barley* and *gram*. The area under principal crops is shown in Table 5.1.

Table 5.1 shows the dominance of wheat and rice crops in gross area sown. The percentage of area under these two crops to the total gross area sown in the state has increased from 28 per cent during 1970-71 to 56 per cent during 2000-01. Though efforts have been made to break dominance of the wheat-paddy rotation, yet no tangible achievement has been made in this regard so far.

The area under wheat is continuously increasing since 1966-67. This area was only 743 thousand hectares in 1966-67. It increased to 1,479 thousand hectares in 1980-81 and jumped to 2,349 thousand hectares in 2000-01. The area under rice was 192 thousand hectares in 1966-67. It increased to 483 thousand hectares in 1980-81 and shot up to 1,049 thousand hectares in 2000-01. The area under total oil seed crops has increased from 211 thousand hectare in 1966-67 to 309 thousand hectares in 1980-81 and further to 415 thousand hectares in 2000-01.

Let us now analyse area under principal crops in various districts of the state. The area is shown in Table 5.2.

Table 5.1

Crop-wise Area of Various Crops in Haryana

(Area in '000 hectares)

Sr. No.	Crops	1966-67	1970-71	1980-81	1990-91	2000-01	2001-02*
(A)	**Kharif**						
(i)	Rice	192	269	483	661	1049	1028
(ii)	Jawar	270	207	136	130	109	104
(iii)	Maize	87	114	71	35	16	
(iv)	Bazra	893	880	871	609	608	608
(v)	Kh. Pulses	38	54	37	68	27	16
Kharif Food grains		**1,480**	**1,524**	**1,598**	**1,503**	**1,809**	1746
(B)	**Rabi**						
(i)	Wheat	743	1,129	1,479	1,850	2,349	2300
(ii)	Gram	1,062	1,063	723	649	77	143
(iii)	Barley	182	109	125	51	48	30
(iv)	Rabi pulses	50	42	36	24	8	9
Rabi Food grains		**2,037**	**2,343**	**2,363**	**2,574**	**2,482**	**2482**
(C)	**Commercials**						
(i)	Sugarcane	150	156	113	148	144	161
(ii)	Cotton	183	194	316	490	555	629
(iii)	Kh. Oil seeds	13	12	10	8	5	4
(iv)	Rabi Oil seeds	198	129	299	474	404	423
(v)	Sun Flower	—	—	—		06	7
Total Oil seeds		**211**	**141**	**309**	**482**	**415**	**424**

*Quick Estimates.

Source: Department of Agriculture, Haryana, Agricultural Statistics at a Glance, 2001, pp. 27-28.

Table 5.2 shows the dominance of wheat and rice crops in most of the districts of the state. Wheat crop occupies the most significant place in cropping pattern of all districts in the state. The concentration of wheat crop was highest in Sirsa followed by Hisar, Jind, Fatehabad, Kaithal, Karnal, Sonipat, Bhiwani, Gurgaon, Faridabad, Kurukshetra, Jhajjar, Rohtak, Panipat respectively.

TABLE 5.2

Area Under Kharif and Rabi Crops in Various Districts of Haryana (2000-01)

(Area In '000 Hectares)

District	*Rice*	*Bajra*	*Maize*	*Wheat*	*Gram*	*Barley*	*Rabi oil seeds*
Hisar	33	58	—	207	05	06	33
Fatehabad	61	10	—	174	02	05	12
Sirsa	40	03	—	244	08	09	27
Bhiwani	08	201	—	137	45	08	108
Rohtak	24	17	—	92	03	02	11
Jhajjar	16	28	—	105	02	04	24
Sonipat	77	08	—	139	—	—	04
Gurgaon	08	65	—	137	01	04	32
Faridabad	29	14	01	134	—	02	04
Karnal	158	03	01	167	01	—	01
Panipat	73	01	—	83	—	—	01
Kurukshetra	112	—	—	109	—	—	—
Kaithal	164	05	—	153	—	—	01
Ambala	72	01	04	78	—	—	01
Panchkula	05	—	08	17	01	—	01
Y. Nagar	56	02	02	62	—	—	01
Jind	112	40	—	207	01	02	04
M.Garh	—	98	—	49	07	02	78
Rewari	1	54	—	55	01	04	54
State	**1049**	**608**	**16**	**2349**	**77**	**48**	**404**

Source: Agricultural Statistics at a Glance, 2001, Department of Agriculture, Haryana, p. 30.

The area under rice is maximum in District Kaithal followed by Karnal, Kurukshetra, Jind, Sonipat, Panipat, Ambala, Fatehabad, Yamuna Nagar, Sirsa, Faridabad, Rohtak, Jhajjar, Bhiwani, Panchkula respectively. The area under bajra, maize, barley, etc. is very less in whole of the state as compared to wheat and rice.

We may mention here that there is limited scope for increasing the cultivable area in the State. The percentage of net area sown to total area of the state has been fluctuating between 81 per cent to 83 per cent since 1984-85. Haryana seems to have reached a saturation point as far as net area sown is concerned. Therefore, agricultural production is being increased through enhanced cropping intensity, change in cropping pattern, improvement in seeds of high yielding varieties and availability of better post-harvest technology. The effective use of bio-fertilizers including vermin compost, phosphatic, solublizing agents and recycling of farm biomass for restoration of soil health and soil productivity, tackling of phalaris minor and other weeds, zero tillage, raised bed planting and precision land leveling methods, adoption of water management technologies, etc. would be disseminated amongst the farmers for higher production projections.

(ii) Agriculture Production

A remarkable increase in agriculture production is visible in Haryana since 1966-67. The trends in agricultural production in the state are shown in Table 5.3.

Table 5.3 shows remarkable increase in production of total food grains (Kharif & Rabi) since 1966-67. Production of total food grains increased from 25.92 lakh tonnes in 1966-67 to 132.50 lakh tonnes in 2000-01, and is estimated at 139.27 lakh tonnes in 2001-02 showing an increase of more than 400 per cent. Wheat and rice played a major role in pushing up the agriculture production. The production of rice was only 2.23 lakh tonnes in 1966-67. It increased to 26.84 lakh tonnes in 2000-01 thereby showing tremendous increase of 1104 per cent. It is estimated at above 27.24 lakh tonnes in 2001-02. Similarly, the production of wheat which was 10.59 lakh tonnes in 1966-67 increased to 96.52 lakh tonnes during 2000-01 showing an increase of 811 per cent. According to quick estimates the production of wheat is estimated to be about 100 lakh tonnes in 2001-02.

The production of cotton and sugarcane during the year 2000-01 rose to 13.83 lakh bales and 8.22 lakh tonnes from 3.05 lakh bales and 5.10 lakh tonnes respectively during 1966-67 recording an increase of 354 per cent and 62 per cent

TABLE 5.3

Crop-wise Production of Various Crops in Haryana

(Production in '000 tonnes/bales of 170 Kg Each.)

Sl. No.	Crops	1966-67	1970-71	1980-81	1990-91	2000-01	2001-02(Q.)
(A)	**Kharif**						
(i)	Rice	223	460	1,259	1,834	2,684	2724
(ii)	Jawar	49	57	48	65	23	22
(iii)	Maize	86	130	81	49	37	47
(iv)	Bazra	373	826	474	526	655	834
(v)	Kharif Pulses	16	27	30	57	14	50
Kharif Food grains		**747**	**1,500**	**1,892**	**2,531**	**3,413**	**3,677**
(B)	**Rabi**						
(i)	Wheat	1,059	2,342	3,490	6,436	9,652	10,000
(ii)	Gram	531	789	455	469	52	100
(iii)	Barley	239	124	181	107	127	140
(iv)	Rabi pulses	16	16	18	16	6	10
Rabi Food grains		**1,845**	**3,271**	**4,144**	**7,028**	**9,837**	**10,250**
Total Food grains		**2,592**	**4,771**	**6,036**	**9,559**	**13,250**	**13,927**
(C)	**Commercials**						
(i)	Sugarcane	510	707	460	780	822	900
(Ii)	Cotton	395	374	643	1,155	1,383	722
(iii)	Kh. Oil seeds	12	9	09	4	02	5
(iv)	Rabi Oil seeds	80	9	178	634	554	650
(v)	Sun Flower	—	—	—	—	09	15
Total Oil seeds		**92**	**98**	**187**	**638**	**565**	**670**

Source: Department of Agriculture Haryana, Agricultural Statistics at a Glance, 2001, pp. 31-32.

respectively. However, according to quick estimates for the year 2001-02 production of cotton is expected to be about 7.22 lakh bales.

It will be interesting to analyse crop-wise production of various crops in terms of various districts of the state. The data is shown in Table 5.4.

TABLE 5.4

Crop-wise Production of Kharif and Rabi Crops in Various Districts of Haryana (2000-01)

(Production in '000 tonnes/bales of 170 kg each)

District	*Rice*	*Bajra*	*Maize*	*Wheat*	*Gram*	*Barley*	*Rabi oil seeds*
Hisar	63	74	—	887	03	19	46
Fatehabad	199	14	—	757	02	16	18
Sirsa	111	03	—	1,015	06	18	51
Bhiwani	20	156	—	451	25	18	128
Rohtak	36	26	—	352	03	5	14
Jhajjar	24	31	—	402	01	12	38
Sonipat	138	12	—	553	—	—	04
Gurgoan	20	78	—	480	1	1	48
Faridabad	80	19	02	539	—	6	06
Karnal	444	03	02	774	1	—	01
Panipat	177	01	—	396	—	—	01
Kurukshetra	357	—	—	506	—	—	01
Kaithal	391	05	—	688	—	—	01
Ambala	217	01	10	272	—	—	01
Panchkula	15	—	19	44	1	—	01
Y. Nagar	167	02	4	230	—	—	01
Jind	222	64	—	895	1	5	05
M. Garh	—	108	—	182	7	6	94
Rewari	3	58	—	228	1	12	96
State	**2,684**	**655**	**37**	**9,652**	**52**	**127**	**554**

Source: Department of Agriculture, Haryana, Agricultural Statistics at a Glance, 2001, p. 33.

The production of rice is highest in Karnal showing 16.54 per cent of total production of State, followed by Kaithal, Kurukshetra, Jind, Ambala, Fatehabad, Panipat, Yamuna Nagar, Sonipat, Sirsa, Faridabad, Hisar, Rohtak, Bhiwani, Gurgaon, Panchkula, Rewari respectively. Mahindragarh shows no production of rice as there is lack of irrigation facilities in district Mahindragarh.

The most important crop of Haryana is wheat, in which the state occupies third place in India after U.P. and Punjab. This crop is cultivated in all districts. Sirsa occupies the first rank producing 10.15 lakh tonnes (10.5% of total production) followed by Jind (8.95 lakh tonnes), Hisar (8.87 lakh tonnes), Karnal (7.74 lakh tonnes) and Fatehabad (7.57 lakh tonnes). On the whole, there are nine districts in the state each of which is producing more than 5 lakh tonnes of wheat every year.

It is also clear from the perusal of Table that rice is grown in all districts of the state except Mahindragarh, Karnal occupies the most important position producing 16.54% share of total production of state; followed by Kaithal (14.56%), Kurukshetra (13.30%), Jind (8.27%), Ambala (8.08%), Fatehabad (7.4%), Panipat (6.59%), Yamuna Nagar (6.22%) and Sonipat (5.14%).

To analyse the growth of agriculture production in Haryana, it is necessary to analyse index of agriculture production in the state. The index is shown in Table 5.5.

TABLE 5.5

Index of Agriculture Production in Haryana

(Base: Triennium ending 1981-82=100)

Year	*Total food grains*	*Total non-grains*	*All commodities*
1980-81	107.02	104.72	106.37
1990-91	164.90	222.27	181.12
1991-92	172.22	249.60	179.12
1992-93	174.59	219.15	185.49
1993-94	186.54	232.11	190.86
1994-95	173.47	252.30	205.14
1995-96	190.91	249.63	195.01
1996-97	189.42	294.50	220.21
1997-98	203.71	185.50	188.23
1998-99	133.35	199.01	202.38
1999-00	214.13	233.76	219.68
2000-01	216.66	234.96	221.84
2001-02	217.93	225.73	220.71
2002-03	201.60	247.05	214.46

Source: Economic Survey of Haryana, 2003-04, p. 91.

Table 5.5 shows that index of agricultural production (Base Triennium ending 1981-82 = 100) has increased from 106.37 in 1980-81 to 221.84 in 2000-01. The index of foodgrain and non-foodgrains have increased from 107.02 and 104.72 in 1980-81 to 216.66 and 234.96 respectively in 2000-01. The index number show remarkable increase in agriculture production leading to almost double during the span of 20 years only. However, the rate of increase has been higher in non-grains as compared to food-grains due to higher profitability in the former.

As a result of higher production of foodgrains, the state of Haryana is one of the largest contributor to food pool. State government is also fully committed to provide remunerative prices and timely support to the farmer by purchasing wheat and paddy at minimum support price on a large scale through a network of 331 purchase centers presently functioning in the state. During 2001-02, the government agencies purchased 64.07 lakh tonnes of wheat and 15.77 lakh tonnes of paddy, which is an all time record.[6]

(b) Yield Pattern of Principal Crops

Yield rate of crops is an important indicator of agricultural development. The yield rate of important crops is shown in Table 5.6.

The Table shows that yield rates of principal crops is quite high. The average yield rate of rice is 2559 kgs. per hectare in the state while on National level the yield rate is 1927 kgs. per hectare. The average yield rate for wheat is 4109 kg. per hectare while at national level it is 2742.

The yield rate of principal crops in terms of various districts of the state is shown in Table 5.7.

The Table 5.7 shows that Sirsa, Bhiwani, Fatehabad, Gurgaon, Faridabad, Karnal, Kurukshetra, Ambala, Panchkula Yamuna Nagar have above state average yield per hectare for rice, whereas the districts of Hisar, Rohtak, Jhajjar, Sonipat, Panipat, Kaithal, Jind have yield below the state average.

In terms of wheat, the districts of Hisar, Fatehabad, Sirsa, Karnal, Panipat, Kurukshetra, Kaithal, Jind, Rewari have yield rate above the state average, while the districts of Bhiwani, Rohtak, Jhajjar, Sonipat, Gurgaon, Faridabad,

TABLE 5.6

Crop-wise Average Yield of Various Crops in Haryana

(Kgs/Hectare)

Crops	*1966-67*	*1970-71*	*1980-81*	*1990-91*	*2000-01*
(A) Kharif					
(i) Rice	1,161	1,697	2,606	2,775	2,559
(ii) Jawar	181	277	354	492	209
(iii) Maize	988	1,142	1,134	1,414	2,339
(iv) Bazra	418	939	544	864	1,077
(v) Kh. Pulses	421	500	811	838	519
Kharif Food grains	**505**	**984**	**1,184**	**1,684**	**1,887**
(B) Rabi					
(i) Wheat	1,425	2,074	2,360	3,479	4,109
(ii) Gram	500	742	629	722	675
(iii) Barley	1,313	1,150	1,451	2,092	2,646
(iv) Rabi pulses	320	381	500	667	750
Rabi Food grains	**906**	**1,396**	**1,754**	**2,630**	**3,963**
Total Food grains	**737**	**1,234**	**1,524**	**2,345**	**3,088**
(C) Commercials					
(i) Sugarcane	737	1234	1524	2345	3088
(ii) Cotton	283	327	346	401	424
(iii) Kh. Oil seeds	899	767	912	500	400
(Iv) Rabi Oil seeds	405	678	597	1338	1371
(v) Sun Flower	—	—	—	—	1500
Total Oils seeds	**435**	**696**	**606**	**1324**	**1361**

Source: Department of Agriculture, Haryana, Agriculture Statistics at a Glance, 2001, p. 29.

Ambala, Panchkula, Yamuna Nagar and Mahindragarh have yield rate below the state average.

It will be interesting to compare the yield rate of principal crops in Haryana with India as a whole as shown in Table 5.8.

TABLE 5.7

Crop-wise Average Yield of Various Crops in Various Districts of Haryana

(Kgs./Hect.)

District	*Rice*	*Bajra*	*Maize*	*Wheat*	*Gram*	*Barley*	*Rabi oil seeds*
Hisar	1,920	1,273	—	4,283	509	3,155	1,394
Fatehabad	3,259	1,356	—	4,351	989	3,181	1,529
Sirsa	2,777	1,037	—	4,161	792	2,042	1,376
Bhiwani	2,559	774	—	3,293	554	2,240	1,215
Rohtak	1,490	1,514	—	3,822	885	2,646	1,315
Jhajjar	1,490	1,110	—	3,826	707	3,112	1,607
Sonipat	1,787	1,475	—	3,986	—	—	1,114
Gurgoan	2,559	1,206	—	3,507	584	2,586	1,499
Faridabad	2,757	1,353	2,339	4,022	—	3,199	1,570
Karnal	2,812	1,077	2,339	4,635	675	—	1,371
Panipat	2,424	1,077	—	4,770	—	—	1,371
Kurukshetra	3,187	—	—	4,641	—	—	—
Kaithal	2,382	1,077	—	4,498	—	—	1,371
Ambala	3,020	1,077	2,525	3,483	—	—	1,394
Panchkula	2,938	—	2,355	2,589	540	—	1,091
Y. Nagar	2,985	1,077	1,901	3,706	—	—	1,010
Jind	1,978	1,595	—	4,324	994	2,646	1,289
M. Garh	—	1,107	—	3,712	957	2,902	1,201
Rewari	2,559	1,069	—	4,153	564	3,081	1,777
State	**2559**	**1077**	**2,339**	**4,109**	**675**	**2,646**	**1,371**

Source: Department of Agriculture Haryana. Agriculture Statistics at a Glance 2001, pp. 29-30

The Table 5.8 shows that although the yield rate of principal crops is quite high while comparing with that of National level but in Haryana, but there is enough scope to increase the yield rates further so as to bring these at per with the best in the world. The power of bio-technology to improve crop yield is today being recognised the world over.

TABLE 5.8

Yield Rates of Principal Crops

(Kgs. per hectare)

Year	*Haryana*		*India*	
	Wheat	*Rice*	*Wheat*	*Rice*
1990-91	3479	2775	2280	1740
1995-96	3697	2225	2483	1797
1996-97	3880	2967	2679	1882
1997-98	3660	2800	2485	1900
1998-99	3916	2239	2583	1928
1999-00	4165	2385	2621	1985
2000-01	4109	2559	2742	1927
2001-02	4103	2652	2770	2086
2002-03	4053	2724	2747	1874

Source: Economic Survey of Haryana, 2003-04, p. 19.

Haryana can take lead in this field by ensuring that research in laboratories reaches the field through extensive services.

(B) Input Indicators and Role of State in Agricultural Development

Progressive agriculture demand, among other things (i.e. favourable institutional and organisation structure), improvement in methods of irrigation; better seeds; better manures and fertilizers; land reclamation and soil conservation; plant protection; use of mechanization, etc. In this context, an attempt has been made to analyse some of the important input indicators, namely:

(i) High yield seed varieties,
(ii) Fertilizers,
(iii) Pesticides,
(iv) Irrigation and flood control,
(v) Mechanisation and use of modern technology, and
(vi) Marketing and Storage.

(i) High Yielding Seed Varieties

Improved strains of seeds are essential for increasing agricultural production. Unless the farmer has good seeds of suitable varieties, he cannot get the best out of other inputs, such as irrigation, fertilizers, insecticide and machinery. With HYV (High Yielding Variety) seeds, it becomes possible for him to take to intensive agriculture because of resultant high yield and good economic returns.

The use of High Yielding variety (HYV) seeds of major crops has increased considerably in the state since its formation in 1966. The area under HYV in the state as a whole and various districts is shown in Table 5.9.

The Table shows that the state has made remarkable progress as far as use of HYV is concerned. In the year 1966-67 there was practically no use of HYV in any of the principal crops in the state, but in the year 1999-2000, 57.2 per cent of total area in rice, 54.7 per cent in maize, 83.5 per cent in bajra and 97.6% in wheat were covered by HYV. As far as various districts of the state are concerned, the ratio of HYV in wheat in almost all the districts was 95% or above. It was 100% in Jind and between 98 to nearly 100% in 10 districts. Similarly in case of rice the ratio of HYV in total area was in excess of 90% in the districts of Panchkula and Rewari while it was more than 70% in Ambala, Yamuna Nagar, Kurukshetra, Sirsa, etc. It leads to the conclusion that still there is great potentiality of increasing the production of rice by improving the rate of HYV. This use of HYV in case of bajra was quite high but it was moderate in maize.

(ii) Fertilizers

The use of chemical fertilizers is now widely accepted as one of the key elements in the strategy for accelerating the growth of agricultural output, especially in short-run. In this context, it is worth-mentioning that fertilizer played a very significant role in enhancing the agricultural productivity and ushering in green revolution in the state. Since the introduction of high yielding varieties, the consumption of chemical fertilizers has been increasing steadily as shown in Table 5.10.

The Table shows that total consumption of NPK

TABLE 5.9

Area Under High Yielding Varieties of Foodgrains in Haryana: 2000-01

(% of The Total Area)
('000 hectares)

District	*Rice*	*Maize*	*Bajra*	*Wheat*
Ambala	73.4	71.4	—	99.5
Panchkula	93.8	49.5	—	95.8
Yamuna Nagar	87.6	71.4	—	99.5
Kurukshetra	78.0	—	—	99.7
Kaithal	55.2	—	85.1	97.8
Karnal	63.8	—	66.7	99.6
Panipat	41.0	—	—	97.7
Sonipat	28.3	—	74.6	98.0
Rohtak	35.1	62.5	88.2	94.6
Jhajjar	40.0	—	80.8	93.8
Faridabad	59.0	—	65.4	99.3
Gurgaon	42.1	—	84.6	89.5
Rewari	90.9	—	82.9	92.8
Mahindragarh	—	—	90.9	99.0
Bhiwani	54.8	—	78.9	94.0
Jind	31.8	—	87.2	100.00
Hisar	44.8	—	92.3	98.8
Fatehabad	75.0	—	93.2	98.8
Sirsa	69.4	54.7	69.0	98.9
State:1966-1967	—	—	—	—
1999-2001	**57.2**	**54.7**	**83.5**	**97.0**

Source: Director of Agriculture, Haryana, Statistical Abstract of Haryana, 2000-2001, p. 241.

(Nutrients) which was only 13,347 tonnes in 1966-67 increased to 70,060 tonnes in 1970-71 and jumped to the level of 9,30,295 tonnes in 2000-01. The trend has been common in case of all types of chemical fertilizers.

Year-wise consumption of fertilizers per hectare of gross area sown in Haryana is given in the Table 5.11.

Table shows that consumption of chemical fertilizers in Haryana has been increasing steadily. It was 42 kg. per hectare in 1981 while in 2000-01 it was 154 kg. per hectare. The per hectare consumption in Haryana is much higher as compared to India as a whole. The per hectare consumption

TABLE 5.10

Fertilizer Consumption in Haryana (Nutrients)

(in tonnes)

Year	*Nitrogenous*	*Phosphatic*	*Potassic*	*Total*
1966-67	12,626	574	147	13,347
1970-71	60,972	6,860	2,228	70,060
1980-81	1,87,385	31,340	12,098	2,30,823
1990-91	4,53,245	13,8005	5,042	5,86,292
2000-01	7,14,308	20,6319	9,668	9,30,295
2001-02	7,42,049	2,32,161	9,750	9,83,960
2002-03	7,20,494	2,50,806	12,298	9,83,598

Source: Director of Agriculture, Haryana, Statistical Abstract of Haryana, 2002-03, p. 269.

TABLE 5.11

Consumption of Fertilizers in Haryana

(in kgs./Hectare)

Year	*Consumption of Fertilizers*
1980-81	42
1990-91	99
1995-96	121
1996-97	125
1997-98	136
1998-99	133
1999-00	150
2000-01	154
2001-02	156
2002-03	164

Source: Economic Survey, Haryana, 2002-03.

of fertilizers in India stood at 112 kg. in the year 2000. However, it must be mentioned here that possibilities of extensive cultivation are extremely limited in Haryana because most of the cultivable area is already being cultivated, there is thus no option but to extend intensive cultivation in more and more areas by using larger quantities of fertilizers (in conjunction with other agricultural inputs) to meet the increasing demand for agricultural commodities.

(iii) Pesticides

One of the problems facing agriculture not only in Haryana, but India as a whole is the loss in agriculture due to weeds, diseases, insects, storage pests, rodent, etc. This points to the need of evolving appropriate plant protection measures. Use of pesticides is one of the steps in this direction. The use of pesticides in Haryana is shown in Table 5.12.

TABLE 5.12

Consumption of Pesticides In Haryana (Technical Grade)

Year	*Quantity in Tonnes*
1966-67	273
1970-71	412
1980-81	2150
1990-91	5165
1999-00	5025
2002-03	4826

Source: Department of Agriculture, Haryana, Agricultural Statistics at a Glance, 2001, p. 191; Statistics Abstract of Haryana, 2002-03, p. 270.

Table shows that consumption of pesticide was 273 tonnes in 1966-67. It increased to 2150 tonnes in 1980-81 and jumped to 5025 tonnes in 1999 - 2000.

As emphasized by Alagh[7] although the importance of pest control measures and the necessity of using pesticides is self-evident, use of pesticides brings with it a number of problems. The first problem is that pesticides are by their very nature poisonous. Accordingly they kill non-target organisms and this includes man. Another problem is that the targeted pests develop resistance towards specific pesticides. The number of species reporting restraint to insecticides has risen to a dozen during the past two decades. Use of fertilizers and pesticides brings about physiological changes in plants leading to multiplication and proliferation of several pests. It is also important to note that pesticides application needs a scientific approach and this approach is lacking in most of our farmers. They are not aware of the actual quantity of toxicant needed to destroy a pest and tend to use more quantity than is necessary. The surplus used appears as a residue that may persist and accumulate within the ecoweb. What is now advocated is not just pest extermination but economical utilization of pesticidal chemicals with least ecological damages.

(iv) Irrigation and Flood Control

Water is one of the major inputs to promote the various sectors of state Economy such as agriculture, industries, animal husbandry, fisheries, forestry, etc. besides catering for the essential requirement of domestic use. According to an estimate, the state of Haryana would be needing about 34 million acre foot (M.A.F.) of water to meet out the annual requirements of all the water consuming sectors by the year 2005 whereas the present level of its availability is only 18.8 M.A.F.[8] Therefore, the need of the hour is to create new resources of water as well as its utilization through an efficient network of canals. The decision of Hon'ble Supreme Court of dated 15th January 2002 for directing the time bound construction of S.Y.L. Canal has come as ray of hope for the water deficient state for which the government was pursuing the case for a long time. This would narrow down the gap between demand and availability of water to some extent.

To make the optimum use of available resources, the state government has been making all out efforts by efficient distribution of water. The internal clearance of irrigation channels is completed prior to the commencement of crop season and all possible steps are being taken to stop the pilferage of water to ensure the supply of canal water to the tail ends. Under Haryana Water Resources Consolidation Project which stands completed by December, 2001, the Government has taken all possible measures for the conservation of water by modernising unlined canals, rehabilitation of old lined canals and replacement of old regulators and other irrigation structures. The main structures replaced/constructed under the project are Hathnikund Barrage along with Link Channel, Pathrala Dam, Ch. Devi Lal Weir at Ottu, Budhera Complex and Sinchai Bhawan which is in advance stage of completion. Canal irrigation of 21.56 lakh hectares and 21.40 lakh hectares respectively was achieved during 1999-2000 and 2000-2001 despite prevailing dry conditions during both the years.[9]

The schemes provided under NABARD projects are meant for better management of water. Since these schemes are in the existing commands and plans have been prepared by adjusting existing *chaks* of various miners to improve upon the efficiency. Besides, providing improved irrigation, it is essential to make more area irrigable by saving it from the flood fury and therefore, some drainage and flood protection schemes for this purpose have also been provided under the NABARD projects. So far NABARD has sanctioned nine projects with total financial outlay of Rs. 394.43 crore out of which NABARD assistance is of Rs. 381.11 crore. The projects consist of 299 irrigation and 212 drainage and flood protection schemes under various trenches of Rural Infrastructure Development Fund (RIDF) loan. Out of these, 170 irrigation and 189 drainage and flood protection schemes have already been completed.[10]

The original capacity of Bhakhra Main Line at the Haryana contact point was 10794 Cs. which came down to 8900 Cs. with the continuous running of canal. The Punjab authorities were persuaded to restore the carrying capacity to its original one. The work of restoration of capacity is in progress for which an amount of Rs. 16.15 crore has been deposited with Punjab Government so far. At present the capacity has come up to 9700 Cs.

This state is being served by the excellent network of irrigation facilities. Canals and tubewells are the main source of irrigation in the state. The status of irrigation facilities available in the state is given in Table 5.13.

The Table 5.13 reveals that gross as well as net area irrigated is continuously increasing in the state since 1966-67.

TABLE 5.13

Irrigation Facilities in Haryana State

('000 Hect.)

Year	*Gross area sown*	*Gross area irrigated*	*%age of gross area irrigated to gross area sown*	*Net area sown*	*Net area irrigated*	*%age of Net Area irrigated to Net area sown*
1966-67	4,599	1,736	37.7	3,423	1,293	37.8
1970-71	4,957	2,230	45.0	3,565	1,532	43.0
1980-81	5,462	3,309	60.6	3,602	2,134	59.2
1990-91	5,919	4,237	71.6	3,575	2,600	72.7
1995-96	5,974	4,673	78.2	3,586	2,760	77.0
1996-97	6,074	4,785	78.8	3,615	2,766	76.5
1997-98	6,143	4,829	78.6	3,635	2,792	76.8
1998-99	6,320	5,041	79.8	3,628	2,842	78.3
1999-00	6,029	5,124	85.0	3,552	2,888	81.3
2000-01	6,045	5,202	86.1	3,526	2,945	83.5

Source: Economic Survey of Haryana, 2001-02, pp. 22-23.

Percentage of gross area irrigated to gross area sown and net area irrigated to net area sown which was 37.8 per cent in the year 1966-67 rose to 86.1 and 83.5 per cent in 2000-2001 respectively. Irrigation intensity during 2000-2001 was 177 in the state. The gross area irrigated in the state will further increase with the completion of S.Y.L. canal.

It will be interesting to analyse the source-wise and cropwise irrigated area in Haryana. The source-wise irrigated area is shown in Table 5.14.

The Table shows that in Haryana, government canals and tubewells are the main source of irrigation. In 1966-67 the area irrigated by government canals was 991 thousand hectares which was 76.64% of total net irrigated area, while in 1999-2000 the area irrigated by government canals was

TABLE 5.14

Source-wise Irrigated Area in Haryana

('000 Hect.)

Year	*Government Canals*	*Tanks*	*Wells*	*Tubewells*	*Other Sources*	*Total*
1966-67	991	4	289	—	9	1,293
1970-71	952	1	574	—	5	1,532
1980-81	1,161	—	26	941	6	2,134
1990-91	1,337	1	—	1,248	14	2,600
1995-96	1,375	1	—	1352	32	2,760
1999-00	1,441	1	—	1,432	14	2,888
2002-03	1,401	1	—	1,507	14	2923

Source: Statistical Abstract of Haryana, 2000-01, p. 269; Economic Survey of Haryana, 2003-04, p. 103.

49.89 per cent of the total. The area irrigated by tubewells in 1999-2000 is 1432 hectares which is 49.58 per cent of total net irrigated area while it was nil in 1966-67. The extensive use of tubewells indicates exhaustive use of underground water resources which has resulted in lowering of water table in Haryana. Crop-wise irrigated area in Haryana is shown in Table 5.15.

TABLE 5.15

Crop-wise Irrigated Area in Haryana

('000 Hect.)

Year	*Rice*	*Jawar*	*Bajra*	*Wheat*	*Maize*	*Gram*	*Other pulses*	*Sugar Cane*	*Cotton*
1966-67	138	72	47	512	23	268	20	127	177
1970-71	235	55	88	914	35	238	15	133	189
1980-81	469	37	103	1,378	17	311	23	103	311
1990-91	655	61	94	1,805	8	141	55	142	488
1999-00	1,081	65	115	2,288	—	43	19	134	541
2001-02	1,026	67	133	2,280	3	39	24	158	627

Source: Statistical Abstract of Haryana, 2002-03, p. 285.

Table 15.5 shows that gross area irrigated has increased in all the major crops. The gross area irrigated in case of rice has increased from 138 thousand hectares in 1966-67 to 1026 thousand hectares in 2001-2002, while in case of wheat it has increased from 512 thousand hectares in 1966-67 to 2280 thousand hectares in 2001-02. In case of cotton the gross area irrigated was 177 thousand hectares in 1966-67 while in 2000-01 it was 627 thousand hectares.

The increase in gross irrigated area in all the major crops indicates extension of irrigation facilities in all the corners of the state, although extensive use of ground water resources is a cause of worry.

The number of tubewells and pumping sets in the state rose from 5,83,705 (2,58,984 diesel operated and 3,24,721 electric operated) in 1999-00 to 5,89,473 (2,55,302 diesel operated and 3,34,171 electric operated) in 2000-01. Additional surface irrigation potential of 4.64 thousand hectares and additional ground water potential of 11.15 thousand hectares was created in the state during 2000-01.

The state government is committed to make Haryana free from the menace of floods which take a heavy toll of life, besides damaging property worth crores of rupees. The state is mainly divided into three drainage tracts, namely, Yamuna Drainage Tract covering of Yamuna Nagar, Kurukshetra (part), Karnal, Panipat, Sonipat, Rohtak (part), Gurgaon and Faridabad (about 37% of the state area), Ghaggar Drainage Tract covering districts of Ambala, Kaithal, Fatehabad, Sirsa and part of Kurukshetra, Jind and Hisar district (about 24% of the state area) and internal drainage tract is spread in the districts of Jind, Bhiwani, Mahindragarh and part of Rohtak and Hisar. As at present no drainage system exists in these districts, hence pumps are used to lift the flood water of this area which is thrown into adjoining drains/canals through a network of small local drains. For this purpose 468 permanent pumping stations have been set-up at various places. In addition, 1450 electric and diesel driven mobile pumps are kept ready to drain out flood waters for immediate relief to the *Abadis* and protecting standing crops. The villages situated in low lying areas have been protected by construction of Ring Bunds and provisions of High level approaches. However, it is proposed to construct Hisar-Ghaggar drain so that flood water can be discharged into river Ghaggar by gravity.[11]

(v) Mechanization and Use of Modern Technology

Land productivity and total agriculture production can be raised substantially through the input of improved seeds and fertilizers. But these inputs become more effective and their potential is better utilized if appropriate mechanization duly supported by the use of modern technology is also made available to the farmers.

A number of field studies have been conducted to determine the relationship between mechanization and productivity. Almost all the studies have indicated that mechanization promotes productivity. The difference between the productivity of a mechanized farm and a non-mechanized farm may range upto as high as between 25 to 30 per cent. The reasons are not far to seek. Depending on the nature of operations, sowing, ploughing fertilization, irrigation and harvesting can be done more efficiently and with less wastage's with the help of machines. For example, the use of machines permits a better distribution of seeds and fertilizers all over the farm than can be achieved in a manual operation.

The use of Agricultural machinery in various districts of Haryana is shown in Table 5.16.

Table 5.16 shows that Karnal district is the most mechanized district as far as use of agricultural machinery is concerned. It had 14,074 Ploughs, 1,895 sugar cane crushers, 34,176 carts, 34,896 tractors, 69,920 tubewells and 2,417 combine harvestors. Panchkula and Mahindragarh are the least mechanized. This because Panchkula is the mostly urban district while Mahindragarh being the agriculturally backward district. As a whole the data reflects extensive use of machinery in various districts reflecting thereby increasing use of modern techniques and rapidly developing agriculture sector.

(vi) Marketing and Storage

Marketing and storage facilities are the crucial components of post-harvest technology. The Haryana state

TABLE 5.16

Agricultural Machinery and Implements in Haryana: 2001

District	*Ploughs*	*Sugarcane crushers*	*Carts*	*Tractors*	*Tubewells*	*Combine harvester*
Ambala	7,942	285	6,852	14,861	22,501	42
Panchkula	5,412	117	1,562	1,094	1,629	84
Y. Nagar	10,170	480	15,649	14,539	27,779	308
Kurukshetra	8,188	150	9,424	11,850	39,981	2,830
Kaithal	27,022	192	27,917	14,007	64,114	1,429
Karnal	14,074	1,895	34,176	34,896	69,920	2,417
Panipat	5,631	538	17,392	7,657	22,917	207
Sonipat	16,317	629	53,717	8,114	78,261	1,806
Rohtak	17,250	140	11,698	4,373	13,482	1,020
Jhajjar	4,310	116	5,401	9,686	19,810	397
Faridabad	2,416	17	49,610	22,844	48,136	13
Gurgaon	7,231	265	3,000	10,222	28,955	661
Rewari	5,179	6	2,651	2,800	41,871	9
Mahindragarh	8,326	5	7,730	8,898	22,361	559
Bhiwani	6,300	551	25,492	11,158	39,238	1,045
Jind	27,835	98	44,461	19,833	38,348	3,793
Hisar	1,32,051	85	60,176	16,023	34,962	1,324
Fatehabad	32,698	68	35,385	22,062	51,763	536
Sirsa	71,785	—	26,568	27,215	44,646	578
State 2001	**4,66,837**	**5,637**	**4,38,861**	**2,62,132**	**7,10,674**	**19,058**

Source: Director of Land Records, Haryana Statistical abstract of Haryana, 2000-01, p. 253.

agricultural marketing board continued its efforts to provide improved and easily accessible market facilities for sale of produce of the farmers in a regulated manner. At the time of creation of the Board in 1969, there were only 58 principal yards and 60 sub-yards in the state. At present, the board has 105 principal yards and 179 sub-yards spread over the state. Average number of villages and area served per market was 64 and 421 sq. kms. respectively in 2000-2001. The total storage capacity of foodgrains (State owned) increased from 16.87 lakh tonnes in 1980-81 to 29.31 lakh tonnes in 2000-01.[12]

The Haryana state agriculture marketing board introduced an incentive scheme, namely, "Krishak Uphar Yojana" from 2nd October, 2000 in all the *mandis* of the State. Under this scheme, prizes in the shape of agricultural implements are being distributed to the farmers who sell their produce worth Rs. 5000 or more in the *mandis* on production of 'J' form issued by the *arthiyas* and in lieu of that they get gift coupons. The aim of this scheme is to encourage the farmers to bring/sell their produce in the *mandis* and to improve the quality of their produce. This scheme has also contributed in increase of market fee and market cess. Under this scheme there are two Ist prizes each of Rs. 40,000, eight 2nd prizes of Rs. 25,000 each and twelve 3rd prizes of Rs. 10,000 each in the shape of agricultural implements. These prizes are distributed in each Kharif and Rabi season in each district. A total sum of Rs. 1.52 crore every year is being awarded under this scheme. Two draws have already been held on 30.04.2001 and 31.10.2001 and agricultural implements amounting to Rs. 76 lakh in each draw have been distributed to the farmers.[13]

IV. DEVELOPMENT OF HORTICULTURE IN HARYANA

Haryana has remained unexploited in the field of horticulture due to major thrust on foodgrain so far. Now, Haryana state is fast emerging as one of the leading states in the field of Horticulture. The state is ideally suited for exploiting the potential of horticulture production due to its close proximity to the metropolitan city of Delhi. Now the main stress has been laid on development of fruits, vegetables, mushrooms, floriculture, etc. with a view to give a boost to the growth of horticulture, special emphasis has been given to the production and supply of good quality nursery fruit plants, from 25 government gardens and nurseries. The area and production under fruits has increased considerably from 12640 hectares and 99.8 thousand tonnes during 1990-91 to 30715 hectares and 232.0 thousand tonnes by the end of 2000-01 respectively. The anticipated achievements of total area and production of fruits for the year 2001-02 are 32815 hectares and 235.0 thousand tonnes respectively. Likewise area and production under vegetables have also increased from 55360 hectares and 802.2 thousand tonnes in 1990-91 to 133000 hectares and 2100.00 thousand tonnes during 2000-01 respectively. Target for the year 2001-02 for area and production under vegetables has been kept as 135000 hectares and 2000.0 thousand tonnes. The commercial flower cultivation has also been taken up at large scale and the area under floriculture has increased from 50 hectares during 1990-91 to 3200 hectares during 2000-01. Target for the year 2001-02 is also 32 thousand hectares. The mushroom production increased from 850 tonnes in 1990-91 to 4200 tonnes by the end of 2000-01 and likely production for 2001-02 has been estimated at 4500 tonnes.[14]

The State Government is also encouraging farmers to adopt Green House Technology for production of off-season vegetables and flowers. 186 Green Houses have so far been established. It is proposed to construct 21 Green Houses during the year 2001-02. The new technologies such as drip and micro-irrigation system are being encouraged to conserve, preserve and utilise the scarce irrigation water. 2699.8 hectares area has been covered under drip and micro-irrigation systems by the end of 2000-01. Target for the year 2001-02 is 360 hectares.

V. DEVELOPMENT OF LIVESTOCK AND POULTRY

Livestock is one of the important components of primary sector of the Economy and there still exists a substantial scope for growth in this sector. The state government is laying emphasis on increasing the production capacity of the animals through genetic improvement of the animals. To minimise production losses efficient health cover facilities are being given through the veterinary institutions. The number of veterinary hospitals and veterinary dispensaries was 579 and 853 respectively in 2001-02 (as on 31-12-2001). The number of stockmen centres/key village centres and regional artificial insemination centres in the states was 751 and 60 respectively during 2001-02 (as on 31.12.2001).

Great stress is also being laid on the improvement of

breed of the cattle and buffaloes to increase the milk yield through artificial insemination with exotic and other improved semen. Haryana Livestock Development Board has been set-up to improve the livestock breed. The central government has sanctioned Rs. 45.00 crore under the National Project for Cattle-Buffalo breeding to improve the quality of livestock.

Haryana is the milk pail of India and is famous for its breed of "Haryana Cows" and "Murrah Buffaloes." To encourage the breeders to maintain their high yielding buffaloes, an incentive scheme has been introduced and incentive money ranging from Rs. 1000 to Rs. 6000 is given to them. Further, to give protection to these animals, insurance schemes has been introduced with 50 : 50 per cent premium from government and breeders respectively.[15]

The milk production in the state has increased to 48.45 lakh tonnes in 2000-01 as against 46.79 lakh tonnes in 1999-2000. The per capita availability of milk in the state has increased from 631 grams per day in 1999-2000 to 637 grams per day in 2000-01. The milk procurement increased in the state from 918.3 lakh litres in 1999-2000 to 1,009.35 lakh litres in 2001-02.

The egg production in the state has increased from 7,589 lakhs in 1999-2000 to 8,007 lakhs in 2000-2001. The production of milk, eggs and wool during the year 1997-98 to 2002-03 are is as under:

TABLE 5.17

Production of Milk, Eggs and Wool in Haryana State

Sl. No.	Item	Unit	Achievements					
			1997-98	1998-99	1999-00	2000-01	2001-02	2002-03
1.	Milk	'000 Tonnes	4,373	4,527	4,679	4,845	4,977	5,125
2.	Eggs	Lakh nos.	6,615	6,825	7,589	8,007	11,668	12,508
3.	Wool	'000 kgs	1,897	1,930	2,202	2,403	2,461	2,498

Source: Economic Survey of Haryana, 2003-04, p. 24.

VI. FISHERIES

There is great potential of fish culture in the state. After green and white revolution, Haryana state is now on the threshold of Blue Revolution also. Fish culture is also being accepted by the farmer of the state as secondary occupation. Farmers have also started construction of fish tanks in their own land as measure of integration of agriculture. The government is providing technical and financial assistance through Fish Farmers' Development Agencies to the fish farmers for fish culture. The fish production increased from 30 thousand tonnes in 1999-2000 to 33.04 thousand tonnes in 2000-01. The state has set a target of 35 thousand tonnes of fish production in 2001-02. Against this, 21.50 thousand tonnes of fish have already been produced upto 31.12.2001 against the National average of 2226 kgs. per hectare of fish production, Haryana has achieved an average production level of 4044 kgs. per hectare during 2000-01 and the state ranks second in the country.[16]

VII. FORESTS

The total area under forests in the state of Haryana is 1.55 lakh hectares which constitutes 2.6 per cent of the total geographical area. Integration of growing tree species along with agricultural crops under agro-forestry, adoption of farm forestry, massive afforestation on degraded panchayat lands and afforestation on mobile sand dunes with active participation of the people has resulted in increase in forest cover of the state by 360 sq. km. over the past two years as reported by forest survey of India in its State of Forest Report 1999. As per National Forest Policy, 1988, 20% area of the total geographical area in plains and 60% in hills should be under forest cover/tree cover for maintaining sound ecological balance.

To meet the growing demand of timber and firewood in the state, it is necessary to rehabilitate the degraded forest areas and bring new areas under forests. To achieve the above objective, afforestation is being carried out under different schemes by forest department. From April, 2001 to

January, 2002, 10081 hectares area has been brought under forest by planting 215.88 lakh plants against the target of 250.00 lakh plants fixed for the financial year 2001-02 under the State/Centrally sponsored schemes. 75.00 lakh plants have been distributed free of cost to various government departments and public for plantation works. To make Haryana State green, government of Haryana has announced a target of 4.5 crore seeding to be planted in the state during the year 2002-03. Government has also announced "Ch. Devi Lal Social Forestry Scheme" to be implemented on strip forests in participation with the farmers of adjoining fields.[17]

VIII. ROLE OF CO-OPERATIVES IN AGRICULTURAL DEVELOPMENT OF HARYANA

Co-operatives have played an important role in the agricultural development of Haryana and improving the economic condition of the people. It has helped in ensuring smooth flow of credit to the agricultural sector, supply of agricultural inputs and arranging for people for marketing of their produce. Initially, the cooperative movement was confined mainly to the field of agriculture credit. Later on, it rapidly spread over to other fields like agro-processing, agro-marketing, rural industries, consumer stores, social services, etc. The progress of disbursement of short-term, medium-term and long-term loans provided by the cooperative societies from 1997-98 to 2001-02 (upto December, 2001) is shown in Table 5.18.

The Table 5.18 depicts that the disbursement of short-term loans was to the tune of Rs. 1865.75 crore in 1999-2000. It increased to Rs. 2957.71 crore in 2000-01. The disbursement of medium-term loans increased from Rs. 15.81 crore in 1999-2000 to Rs. 115.41 crore in 2000-01. The disbursement of long-term loans increased from Rs. 253.01 crore in 1999-2000 to Rs. 281.50 crore in 2000-01. The targets for 2001-02 is to disburse Rs. 2889.79 crore short-term loans, Rs. 284.11 crore medium-term loans and Rs. 355.67 crore long-term loans. Against these targets, Rs. 1985.01 crore have been disbursed under short-term loans, Rs. 52.77 crore under medium-term loans and Rs. 249.14 crore under long-term loans upto December, 2001.

TABLE 5.18

Progress of Short-Term, Medium-Term and Long-Term Loans Disbursed by Cooperative Societies

(Rs. in crore)

Type of Loan	*Loan Disbursed*				*2001-02*	
	1997-98	*1998-99*	*1999-00*	*2000-01*	*Target*	*Loan Disbursed upto 31.12.2001*
Short-Term	1,243.88	1,508.00	18,675.75	2,957.71	2,889.79	1,985.01
Medium-Term	8.98	39.00	15.81	115.41	284.11	52.77
Long-Term	228.40	243.68	253.01	281.50	355.67	249.14

Source: Economic Survey of Haryana, 2001-02, p. 20.

Twelve co-operative sugar mills are functioning in the State with a total crushing capacity of 25,050 tonnes daily. Two new mills "Ch. Devi Lal Coop. Sugar Mills" in Sirsa and Sonipat have started their operations this year. In the year 2001-02, sugar mills crushed 342.68 lakh quintals of sugar cane and produced 32.83 lakh quintals sugar. Sugar mills have been in the forefront for making competitive cane price payment in the State and the payment of price to the cultivators is much higher than the statutory minimum cane price fixed by Government of India during the year 2001-02. The prices fixed by the State Government are Rs. 104, Rs. 106 and Rs. 110 per quintal for different varieties of cane in the State and it is understood that these are highest in the entire country.[18]

IX. PROBLEMS AND SUGGESTIONS FOR AGRICULTURAL DEVELOPMENT IN HARYANA[19]

After analysing the trend of agricultural development in Haryana it is logical to discuss the main problems and to suggest remedial measures. In this context, some important problems are as follows:

(i) Soil and Water Problem

Creation of intensive irrigation facilities and excessive

use of canal water have resulted in the problems of water-logging, soil salinity and soil solidity. The other factors contributing to the rise of these soil problems include impeded drainage, topography, salt-laden parent material, poor water management practices, poor quality of ground water and above all arid to semi-arid climatic conditions. Wind erosion and frequent flooding, excessive permeability of sandy soils, soil conservation and high calcareous nature of soils are some other additional solid problem encountered in Haryana.

Due to these problems, the production and productivity in the State is suffering resulting in heavy losses to the agricultural sector. Owing to the mismanagement of irrigation water, there are instances where irrigation, instead of being a blessing has become a curse especially, in arid and semi arid areas where natural drainage is inadequate and an artificial drainage is not provided. It is estimated that about 1900 sq. km. land area is affected by problem of salinity in Haryana. Out of this, 650 sq. km. is very severely affected by high salinity and the problem to lesser extent affects about 1140 sq. km. of the total area of the state. In Haryana roughly 3310 sq. km. (7.5 per cent of the total area) is affected by soldicity or alkalinity. Out of this 2090 sq. km. is with strong soldicity problem.[20] Problem areas of soldicity are mostly confined with mean annual rainfall ranges of 550 to 1000 mm. Water-logging is wide-spread problem in the state due to peculiar geographic setting of the state which does not provide much natural drainage. As stated above, the genesis of water-logging and salinity in Haryana is mainly due to its geographical location farmers of the affected districts reported that there was no such problem till the late sixties. The problem gradually started creeping in the area with the introduction of canal irrigation. Drainage system has been tried at various places. The cost of drainage per hectare varies from place to place depending on the soil type, spacing between lateral drains, quality of drain pipe, depth of drains, size of drainage basin, installation cost of sub-surface drainage, etc. Due to this problem their is need of creation of surface and sub-surface drainage system and correcting water imbalances in good and bad regions in the state.

(ii) Agrarian Structure

Eroding base of agricultural sector under the impact of sub-division and fragmentation of holdings is the most important limiting factors for making further investment in durable assets. At the same time it also hinder the free competition in the market. Over 76 per cent of the land holdings in India are below one hectare. Further, more than two-third of these holdings are below 0.5 hectares. These holdings cover about 30 per cent of the total operated area. The situation as prevailing at India level also holds good for Haryana agriculture. Number and area of holdings by ownership and by size of group in Haryana State is given in Table 5.19.

TABLE 5.19

Number and Area of Holdings by Ownership and by Size of Group in Haryana State

(Area in Hectares)

Size Group (in Hectares)	*Number*	*Area*	*Number*	*Area*
Below 0.5	1,87,966	56,932	4,79,463	1,49,380
0.5-1.0	1,37,559	1,08,117	3,35,196	2,54,775
1.0-2.0	1,94,079	3,05,213	3,38,446	4,73,042
2.0-3.0	1,23,478	3,09,176	1,96,526	4,68,492
3.0-4.0	87,387	3,12,694	1,31,941	4,47,061
4.0-5.0	67,131	2,99,795	83,478	3,75,067
5.0-7.5	98,133	6,15,150	81,411	4,97,488
7.5-10	50,898	4,32,797	41,469	3,49,876
10-20	53,467	7,49,811	32,435	4,31,635
20 & above	11,466	3,71,989	7,628	2,28,911
Total	**10,11,564**	**35,61,674**	**17,27,993**	**36,75,727**

Source: Department of Agriculture, Haryana, Agricultural Statistics at a Glance, 2001, p. 5.

The Table reveals that in 1980-81 about 73% of holdings were less than 4 hectares while in 1995-96 the ratio increase to about 86%. The small holdings are dismaliy small, highly fragmented and economically unviable. They are incapable of operating on commercial scale/business line. They can neither fully absorb new technology nor they can withstand the competition envisaged in new economic policy.

The basic objective of the proposed agrarian structure should be that these Agricultural holdings must be economically viable to support the family and have marketable surpluses for further investment. With this basic objective in mind the appropriate steps suggested can be:

(1) The size of a farm holding should be decided which is economically viable in different agro-climatic zones and the ceiling laws should be formulated accordingly.
(2) In order to enable the farm units to grow upto the viable size long-term and low interest loans may be provided against mortgage of land as collateral. This will create vast land market and small units will start disappearing.
(3) The persons who sell their land should be provided all facilities to invest in the agro-industries by the financial institutions and the government.
(4) Farm units of viable size should be treated as industrial/commercial enterprises that should invite all the provisions of industrial laws and regulations.

(iii) Value Addition and Exports

There is tremendous potential for increasing exports of agricultural land agro-based products both in the traditional and the new international markets by the state. The emerging commodities are rice, durum wheat, horticultural crops, vegetables, dairy products, floriculture crops, vegetables, dairy products, floriculture. The state is surplus in rice, wheat, cotton and floriculture. The package required in this direction should be:

(1) Strict quality control and standards.

(2) Investment in export infrastructure and marketing assets.
(3) Cost and price competitiveness of these products.
(4) Credit facilities to the exporters.
(5) Exploration of markets which have remained unexplored hitherto.
(6) Incentive packages for inflow of capital in export sector both for foreign and domestic capital.

(iv) Subsidisation of Agricultural Sector

Gradual withdrawal of subsidies is an important plank of new economic policy. Subsidisation of inputs and output was done indiscriminately irrespective of target groups of farming community. Consequently, there was the little percolation of benefits to the small and marginal farmers as it was significantly siphoned off by the big farmers. A group of vested interests developed and the burden on public exchequer increased leading to budget deficits and inflation. The pricing of these inputs and output developed a lot of distractions and irrationalities. In an Economic of privatisation, liberalisation and globalisation, there is need of the market Economic of demand and supply. The subsidization policy should follow the following names:

(1) Withdrawal of subsidies should be gradual with a given time frame.
(2) These should be properly targeted so that it reaches the target groups.
(3) These should provide incentives to produce and market more.
(4) These should be rationalized to reflect market demand and supply.

(v) Changes in Cropping Pattern

There is also need to change the existing cropping pattern because it is not optimal. At present we are faced with surplus of some crops and deficit in others. Therefore, there is need to have a balanced growth in crops to bring about an equilibrium between demand and supply, higher rate of return and optimum resource allocation. Area under wheat will have to be restricted whereas the productivity will have to be raised. Rate of growth of production of rice, pulses, oilseeds, sugarcane and cotton has to be accelerated.

Experience shows that every increase in irrigation area goes to wheat and rice. Therefore, there is need to change the production technology of oilseeds and pulses to attract irrigated area under these crops. This will involve review of various policy issues in terms of rationalisation of water rates, price policy and the incentives and disincentive to manipulate are under various crops.

(vi) Research and Development

The future growth of agriculture sector will largely depend on the investment made in research and development. Unfortunately, the country is spending an insignificant percentage of total GDP in research in agriculture. If we have to compete in the world and bring about break-through in agriculture, investment on agricultural R & D must be stepped up tremendously. At present our agricultural R & D institutions are facing severe resource crunch which does not augur well for future agricultural development.

The above mentioned issues are only a few. Many more issues are awaiting immediate solution. Therefore, there is need of a well integrated perspective planning for policy framework.

Notes and References

1. Simon Kuznets, "Six lectures on Economic Growth", p. 6.
2. Statistical Abstract of Haryana, 2000-01, p. 191.
3. *Ibid.*, p. 229.
4. Subrata Ghatak and Ken Ingresent: Agriculture and Economic Development, p. 69.
5. Statistical Abstracts of Haryana and Punjab, 1966.
6. Economic Survey of Haryana, 2001 - 02, p. 14.
7. Y.K. Alagh, Pesticides in Indian Agriculture, *EPW*, September 17, 1998, p. 1959.
8. Economic Survey of Haryana, 2001-02, p. 21.
9. *Ibid.*
10. *Ibid.*, p. 22.

11. *Ibid.*, p. 23.
12. *Ibid.*, p. 16.
13. *Ibid.*
14. *Ibid.*, p. 17
15. *Ibid.*
16. *Ibid.*, p. 19.
17. *Ibid.*
18. *Ibid.*, p. 21.
19. S.D. Chamola, Agriculture Development Project for Haryana, Directorate of Research CCS, HAU, Hisar.
20. *Ibid.*

6

EMERGING PATTERN OF INDUSTRIAL DEVELOPMENT

I. INDUSTRIAL DEVELOPMENT—AN INTRODUCTION

Development literature frequently emphasizes the importance of a strong agricultural base for developing countries. A top priority to agriculture is always recommended in these cases and manifold gains emanating from agricultural development are highlighted: employment to multitude of people, self-reliance in food production, provision of industrial raw materials and generation of surplus resources for other sector of Economy.

There is, however, a limit to which agriculture can develop itself. It has to be supported by a vibrant industrial sector for a sustained economic growth. Prof. P.C. Mahalanobis believed that the developing countries may initially give a priority to agriculture to gain self-reliance but soon they should shift the emphasis to industry so as to benefit from its multiplier effects. For agricultural development itself, industrialization is vital.[1]

Hirschman (1958) advocates industrialization on the ground that it generates backward and forward linkages in regional Economic. Not only it stimulates a demand for several industrial inputs but also promotes several activities based on industrial output. This type of structural transformation of an Economy is a necessary condition for cumulative and self-sustaining growth.[2]

Murray D. Bryce has also stated that "Industrial development has a necessary and ultimately a large role to play in almost any sound development programme.[3]

Finally, in the words of Late Pt. Jawahar Lal Nehru "The God, which all the countries worship is the God of industrialisation, the God of machine, the God of high production and utilisation of natural power and resources for greater advantage."[4]

For us, it is imperative here to examine the industrialisation process in Haryana after having analysed its agricultural development of special interest will be the fact of its recent formation as impinging upon the industrial policy and progress.

II. HARYANA INDUSTRIALISATION: PRE-FORMATION SCENE

Till 1966, location, structure and organisation of Haryana's industrialisation were an integral part of industrial development in the former Punjab. The Haryana territory could not boast of a strong industrial base at that time.

Earlier before independence in 1947, the industrial scene was defined by indigenous handicraft and cottage industries in rural areas and a few British owned large and medium scale industries in cities. Industrial development was of low and sporadic nature. This was in tune with the British policies, which emphasized export of raw materials and import of finished goods rather than establishment of manufacturing units.

Just before independence, only five per cent of the factories registered in the provinces of India were located in the Indian Punjab. The employment share worked out to 1.5 per cent of the 572 factories registered in the region 187 were located in Amritsar district, 78 in Ludhiana district and 63 in Jalandhar district. Among the districts now in Haryana, Ambala had the highest number of 49 units while the share of other districts was very small.[5]

Haryana territory was comparatively not so

unfavourably placed in respect of large and medium scale industry. The Amritsar-Calcutta and Amritsar-Bombay railways traversing through this area were of some help. In 1947, the Haryana territory accounted for 18 units out of 44 in the then Punjab. These were distributed among 8 centres. The distribution of large and medium scale industry in Haryana in 1947 is shown in Table 6.1.

TABLE 6.1

Haryana: Distribution of Large and Medium Scale Industry in 1947

District	*Industrial Centres*	*Number of Units*
Ambala	Ambala (2), Jagadhri (1), Y. Nagar (5), Surajpur (1)	9
Bhiwani	Bhiwani (2), Dadri (1)	3
Faridabad	Faridabad (5)	5
Gurgaon	—	—
Hisar	—	—
Jind	—	—
Karnal	—	—
Kurukshetra	—	—
M. Garh	Rewari (1)	1
Rohtak	—	—
Sirsa	—	—
Sonipat	—	—
Total		18

Source: Directory of Large and Medium Industries of Haryana, Directorate of Industries, Haryana, Chandigarh.

The Table shows that out of total 18 units, 9 units were located in district Ambala while Faridabad, Bhiwani and Mahindragarh had 5, 3, and 1 unit respectively. All other districts had no medium or large scale industry. This signifies the backwardness of Haryana territory with regard to large and medium scale industry.

Some of the important industrial centers in Haryana territory included Panipat (Woolen Goods/Blankets, Brass

Metalwares and Pottery), Bhiwani (Cotton ginning and Textiles), Ambala (Cotton rugs or Dairies), Karnal (Bottles glasses, Mirrors, Lamps and Chimneys), Jagadhri (Brass utensils), Rewari (Utensils) and Jhajjar (Unglazed pottery). Many of the manufactured goods were for supply to the army as also for meeting the requirements of the regional market.

In respect of small-scale industry, the position of Haryana territory was indeed poor. It shared only about nine per cent of such units in the then Punjab. Even by the end of 1950, the now Punjab territory had 1,624 units and Haryana territory only 484 units. Ambala district, in Haryana territory alone claimed 366 units.[6] It shows that the Haryana territory was not only industrially backward but most of its industries were confined to a few districts and this also at some places within them.

The initial impact of the partition of the Indian sub-continent was negative for the former Punjab, including Haryana territory, for two reasons. First, whatever industry had developed by then was damaged during the then communal riots. Secondly, migration of large number of muslim artisans, who constituted the skilled labour, to Pakistan led to virtual closure of several factories and workshops, thereby creating a vacuum in the region's industrial activities.

A fresh start had to be made in industrialisation after partition. Industrial development of Punjab is, in a sense, recent history. It started mostly with the courageous efforts of people who tried to build on what was left of the wrecks of partition. The government encouraged establishment of industries at places like Nilokheri, Faridabad, Bahadurgarh, Sonipat, Panipat, Jagadhri, Ropar and Khanna during 1948-50.

It needs to be added that a base for rapid industrialisation of now Haryana was laid soon after independence. Its two main assets included a relatively distant location from the international border and proximity to the national capital of Delhi. The settlement of enterprising displaced person in the planned industrial estates provided an additional impetus to the process.

In spite of all this at the time of its formation in 1966,

Haryana lagged behind Punjab as far as industrial scenario is concerned. Table 6.2 is testimony to this.

TABLE 6.2

Haryana and Punjab: A Comparative Picture of Some Indicators of Industrial Development, 1966

Indicator	*Ratio between Haryana and Punjab*
Number of Registered Factories*	1: 3.03
Number of Registered Factories per lakh of Population	1: 2.45
Number of Small-Scale Units**	1: 4.29
Consumption of Electric Power by Industries	1: 1.33
Investment in Central Public Sector Projects	1: 4.58

* All Industrial Establishments, Small-Scale or Large-Scale, Registered with the Inspector of Factories in each state under the Factories Act, 1948, are called 'factories'. All industrial units employing 10 or more workers and using power or 20 or more workers when not using power are required to get them registered under the Factories Act.

** These include all industrial units with a capital investment (plant and machinery) of not more than Rs. 0.75 million, irrespective of the number of persons employed; the ceiling prior to October 1966 was Rs. 0.50 million (Government of India, 1970).

Sources: (i) Government of Punjab (1966): Final Report, Haryana Development Committee, Chandigarh.

(ii) Report of the Industrialists' committee on Intensive Industrialisation of Haryana, 1969, p. 3.

Table 6.2 shows that ratio of registered factories between Haryana and Punjab was 1: 3.03 while the ratio of small-scale industry was 1: 2.45. The investment in central public sector units was also in favour of Punjab (1: 4.58).

It follows from above discussion that Haryana territory of composite Punjab, though enjoying locational advantage in respect of industry was lagging behind Punjab in all spheres of industrial activities. In the year 1966, the total number of small-scale units in Haryana was 4519 while that of large and medium scale industry was 162.[7] There was only one public sector unit in Haryana that was unit of Hindustan Machine Tools (HMT) in Pinjore, which was established in the year 1962. The total number of small-scale units is shown in Table 6.3.

TABLE 6.3

Number of Small-Scale Enterprises in Haryana (Nov. 1966)

Districts	*No. of Units*
Ambala	1752
Karnal	584
Faridabad	454
Gurgaon	368
Rohtak	333
Sonipat	327
Kurukshetra	215
Jind	200
Bhiwani	126
Mahindragarh	77
Hisar	53
Sirsa	53
Total	**4,519**

Source: Udyog Yug, July 1985, p. 97.

The Table 6.3 shows that the Ambala district with 1752 units dominated the small-scale scenario in 1966. Karnal, Faridabad and Gurgaon followed it with 584, 454 and 368 units respectively. Hisar and Sirsa districts had least number of small-scale units, i.e. 53 each.

III. POST-FORMATION SCENE OF INDUSTRIAL DEVELOPMENT IN HARYANA

Let us now reflect as to how the formation of Haryana as a new state was to influence its industrial development. The following was visualized for the state in this regard:

(i) It could pursue an autonomous industrial policy including matters relating to its structure (small or large-scale industries), organisation and location.

(ii) It could locate new industrial estates or identify industrially backward districts/areas for special care.

(iii) It could reap the advantage of its proximity to Delhi with greater intensity.

In addition, the new agricultural prosperity in the wake of green revolution ushering in around that time was also to make its own impact on the industrial scene of the state.

The basic indicators for the measurement of economic development of an Economic in Haryana are expressed in terms of Net State Domestic Product (sector-wise) over a period of time. This helps us to know how the industrial sector has grown over this period of time. Table 6.4 shows the sector-wise Net Domestic Product at factor cost (current price) in Haryana from 1966-67 to 2000-01.

TABLE 6.4

Sector-wise Net Domestic Product in Haryana at Factor Cost (Current Prices)

(Rs. in crores)

Years	*Primary Sector*	*Secondary Sector*	*Tertiary Sector*	*Total*
1966-67	356.23 (67.21)	79.43 (14.98)	94.39 (17.81)	530.05
1980-81	1,655.46 (54.65)	575.37 (18.55)	801.12 (26.79)	3,031.95
1993-94	8,315.72 (42.79)	4,931.31 (24.27)	6,174.52 (32.94)	19,421.55
1994-95	9,617.65 (42.88)	6,298.69 (24.86)	7,219.95 (32.25)	23,136.29
1995-96	9,668.34 (39.74)	8,110.57 (26.42)	8,386.67 (33.84)	26,165.58
1996-97	12,006.86 (35.53)	9,021.34 (26.99)	10,316.83 (35.27)	31,345.03
1997-98	11,867.40 (35.00)	10,177.35 (30.00)	11,865.53 (35.00)	33,910.28
1998-99	13,408.12 (35.02)	11,074.55 (28.92)	13,805.81 (36.06)	38,288.40
1999-00	14,215.96 (31.46)	12,231.66 (28.79)	16,040.01 (37.75)	42,487.63
2000-01	14,923.70 (31.44)	13,488.45 (28.41)	19,061.63 (40.15)	47,473.78
2002-03*	15,510.39 (26.77)	16,487.15 (28.46)	25,939.00 (44.77)	57,937.49

*Quick Estimates.

Note: Figures in Parentheses are percentages to the total.

Source: Statistical Abstract of Haryana, various issues.

Table 6.4 reveals that in 1966-67, the primary sector comprising of agriculture and animal husbandry, forestry and logging, fishing, mining and quarrying accounted for Rs. 356.23 crores of Net Domestic Product. This value increased to Rs. 1,655.46 crores in 1980-81 and went on increasing further till it touched the highest level of Rs. 14,923.70 crores in 2000-01. However, in relative terms, the share of primary sector in total Net Domestic Product of Haryana has a declining trend during this period. It declined from 67.21 per cent in 1966-67 to 54.65 per cent in 1980-81 and only to 31.44 per cent in 2000-01.

The secondary sector, which comprises of manufacturing units (registered or unregistered), construction, electricity, gas and water supply accounted for Rs. 79.43 crores in 1966-67, which increased to Rs. 575.37 crores in 1980-81 before touching on all time high mark of Rs. 13,488.45 crores in 2000-01. Thus, the value of Net Domestic Product in Secondary sector increased significantly during the period from 1966-67 to 2000-01. In relative terms also, the share of the secondary sector in the total Net Domestic Product has increased over the period. It was only 14.98 per cent in 1966-67 and increased to 18.55 per cent in 1980-81 and to 28.41 per cent in 2000-01.

The tertiary sector, which comprises of transport, storage and communication, trade, banking, insurance and other services accounted for Rs. 94.39 crores in 1966-67. This value increased to Rs. 801.12 crores in 1980-81 and to Rs. 19,061.63 crores in 2000-01. The relative share of tertiary sector in total Net Domestic Product was just 17.81 per cent in 1966-67, which increased to 26.79 per cent in 1980-81 and to 40.15 per cent in 2000-01. This means that there is an increasing trend of tertiary sector also over the previous years.

Thus, the sector-wise trend of growth in Haryana reveals that the share of primary sector in total Net Domestic Product has decreased during these years. It shows the declining importance of agriculture as is expected in growing Economic due to application of:

(1) Engel's Law, and
(2) Growing Relative Productivity.

These two reasons present a paradoxical situation in which both the agricultural production and the productivity are increasing on the one hand and on the other, the relative contribution of this sector is declining. The share of secondary sector has shown an increasing trend upto 1997-98 but after that it has been stabilised. However, the share of tertiary sector has shown a significant increase and that too continuously.

IV. PATTERN OF INDUSTRIALISATION

Rapid industrial growth has been accepted as an essential condition for accelerated rate of growth. The policy aiming at rapid industrialisation is based on industrial potential survey, which presents "Comprehensive knowledge of the existing industries and ways and means to develop these on the one hand, and measures for establishment of new enterprises on the other."[8]

The importance of industrialisation as a means of achieving rapid growth and prosperity has long been recognised since the inception of Haryana. It is emerging at a frontline state towards industrial growth. A systematic planning of its industrial activity and sustained promotion of new enterprises in an atmosphere of harmonious industrial relations have contributed significantly to the achievement of present high level of industrialisation in the state. Phenomenal growth of industries in Haryana during the recent past has also attracted the attention of all interested in industrial geography.

The industrial growth in Haryana has been marvellous in all spheres of industrial activities. Its progress within short span of 36 years (1966-2001) has been remarkable. During the past three and half decades, the number of registered factories and the number of persons employed in the industrial sector shot upto 8,631 and 4,98,656 respectively in the year 2000 from the corresponding figure of 900 and 64,564 in 1966.

The proximity of Haryana to Delhi, the nation's capital has acted as greatest stimulant for the rapid growth of industries in the state. Delhi is one of the biggest market for both wholesale and retail trade. Since most of the areas in Haryana are at a stone's throw from the nation's capital, they are reaping the fruits of its situational advantage.

Like all economic growth, industrial growth depends upon "certain pre-conditions whose fulfilment in varying degrees dictates the place and pattern of industrial expansion."[9] Among the factors which constitute the infrastructure of growth, some are economic while others are non-economic in nature. Among the economic pre-conditions of growth are adequate basic facilities of transport and communication, power, technical skills, banking and financial organisations and so on. The non-economic factors vary from political stability and growth-oriented administration to social and cultural heritage. Here we need not go into the whole complex of the socio-economic overheads of economic development. For the purpose of analyzing industrial development of Haryana, we are concentrating on three major economic conditions, which are directly related to the process of industrialisation of Haryana.

(a) Growth in number of registered units and workers employed therein.
(b) Contribution of constituents of industrial sector to Net Domestic Product of Haryana.
(c) Growth in the Industrial Production.

(a) Growth in Number of Registered Units and Workers Employed Therein

Haryana has shown unprecedented growth of industries in industrially backward as well as in developed areas. On the whole, the manufacturing sector recorded a creditable average annual growth rate of 7.1 per cent during 1966-2000. by comparison the overall economic growth rate was 5.60 per cent per annum.[10] The state Domestic Product from manufacturing (registered and unregistered) grew from Rs. 703 crores to Rs. 9781.76 crores over the period.

Table 6.5 shows the number of registered working factories and number of workers employed in these factories during the period 1966-2000.

Table 6.5 shows the number of registered factories increased from 900 in 1966 to 8,804 in year 2002. There was corresponding rise in industrial employment from 64,564 to 5,40,338 over the corresponding period.

TABLE 6.5

Haryana: Number of Registered Factories and Number of Workers Employed

Year	*Number of Working Registered Factories*	*Number of Workers Employed*
1966	900	64,564
1970	1,359	88,675
1975	1,791	1,09,834
1980	3,176	1,75,025
1985	4,484	2,26,476
1990	4,843	2,69,411
1995	6,498	3,91,386
1998	7,813	4,44,911
1999	8,292	4,71,152
2000	8,631	4,98,656
2001	8,804	5,19,663
2002	8,974	5,40,338

Source: Various issues of Statistical Abstract of Haryana from 1966 to 2002.

Table 6.6 gives district-wise data of registered working factories and number of workers employed. The Table 6.6 shows that first four ranking districts, i.e. Faridabad, Gurgaon, Ambala (including Yamuna Nagar) and Karnal accounted for 70.44 per cent of total units in 1966 and 67.60 per cent of number of workers employed. In the year 1966 maximum number of registered units were located in Ambala district (272). Though this number reached to 403 in the year 2000, its rank has gone down to 7th place.

In the year 1966 the second position was held by Faridabad with 205 units, but in the year 2000 Faridabad was occupying first position with 2,471 units. Gurgaon district has also shown remarkable increase from merely 47 units in 1966 to 926 units in 2000, it occupying third position after Yamuna Nagar district. The Yamuna Nagar district, which was part of Ambala district in 1966 occupied second position in the year 2000 on the basis of 1,184 units. Compared to these districts

Table 6.6

District-wise Number of Registered Factories and Workers Employed

Districts	Number of Units		% Increase over 1966	No. of Workers Employed		% Increase over 1966
	1966	2000		1966	2000	
Ambala	272	403	48.16	15,190	14,362	(-) 5.45
Bhiwani	12	115	858.33	4,769	12,869	169.84
Faridabad	205	2,471	1105.36	21,039	1,77,778	744.99
Gurgaon	47	926	1870.21	4,032	79,199	1,864.26
Hisar	58	347	498.27	4,404	12,166	1,762.48
Jind	9	156	1633.33	248	6,184	2,393.54
Karnal	110	437	297.27	4,365	26,779	513.49
Kurukshetra	29	165	468.96	762	3,163	315.09
M. Garh	6	60	900	352	4,250	1,107.38
Rohtak	70	225	221.42	4,182	13,169	214.89
Sirsa	34	123	261.76	1,303	6,788	420.95
Sonipat	48	530	1004.16	3,918	28,590	629.7
Panchkula	—	127	—	—	9,826	—
Y. Nagar	—	1,184	—	—	37,587	—
Kaithal	—	123	—	—	2,710	—
Panipat	—	682	—	—	29,467	—
Jhajjar	—	311	—	—	16,891	—
Rewari	—	130	—	—	13,188	—
Fatehabad	—	116	—	—	3,690	—
Total	900	8,631	859.00	64,564	4,98,656	686.85

Source: Statistical Abstract of Haryana (2000-01), p. 375.

Mahindragarh, Kaithal, Fatehabad are industrially backward as far as registered manufacturing units are concerned, having only 60,123 and 116 units respectively.

Taking employment into consideration, we see that in 1966 Faridabad and Ambala were top two districts with 21,039 and 15,190 workers employed in registered working factories in these two districts respectively. In 2000, Faridabad occupied first position by providing employment to 1,77,778 workers, while Gurgaon was at the second place employing 79,199 workers.

Let us now analyse the industry-wise growth in registered factories during the period 1966 to 2000. The growth is depicted in Table 6.7.

The Table 6.7 shows that in 1966, metal and metal products industry dominated with 162 units followed by cotton textile and textile products industry with 156 units and food products and beverage industries, which had 115 units. In the year 2000, cotton textile and textile products occupied first position with 1,560 units followed by metal and metal products and non-metallic mineral products with 994 and 960 units respectively.

Taking employment into consideration we see that, in 1966 cotton textile industry topped in providing employment to 14,085 workers. Transport equipment, machinery and machine tools ranked second and third respectively with 8,649 and 8,350 workers employed. In the year 2000 machinery and machine tools industry ranked first in providing employment to 95,727 workers, the second place is occupied by cotton textile industry, which is providing employment to 69,972 workers. The highest percentage change in employment, i.e. 3,624.34 per cent took place in chemical and chemical product industry. Non-metallic mineral industry experienced remarkable percentage change of 1,294.87 per cent, while rubber, plastic and petroleum product experienced 1,760.58 per cent change over 1966.

Thus, it follows from above analysis that diversification of industries has occurred in the manufacturing sector in terms of both the number of units as well as number of workers employed therein. It is also clear that processing industries like machinery and machine tools, cotton textiles, basic metal, metal products and parts dominated the industrial scene of manufacturing activity. Ambala, Faridabad, Gurgaon and Yamuna Nagar districts have dominated the manufacturing sector not only in terms of registered units, but also in terms of workers employed, while Panchkula, Fatehabad and Kaithal districts are lagging behind as far as registered working factories are concerned.

TABLE 6.7

Industry-wise Growth of Manufacturing Activity in Haryana

Industries	*Number of Units*		*% Increase over 1966*	*Number of Workers Employed*		*% Increase over 1966*
	1966	*2000*		*1966*	*2000*	
Food Products, Beverage & Tobacco	115	809	603.48	5,230	31,803	508.08
Cotton Textile & Textile Products	156	1,560	900	14,085	69,972	396.78
Wood & Wood Products	39	294	653.85	1,569	11,796	651.82
Paper & Paper Products	21	252	1,100.00	3,515	17,142	387.68
Leather & Leather Products	—	131	—	—	10,348	—
Rubber, Plastic & Petro Products	24	473	1,870.83	1,535	28,560	1,760.58
Chemical & Chemical Products	24	528	2,100.00	760	28,305	3,624.34
Non-Metallic Mineral Products	11	960	8,627.27	3,101	43,255	1,294.87
Basic Metal & Alloy Industry	58	753	1,198.28	3,675	43,439	1,082.01
Metal & Metal Products	162	994	5,130.58	4,744	34,225	621.43
Machinery & Machinery Tools	125	677	441.6	8,350	95,727	1,046.43
Electrical Machinery	63	363	476.19	4,452	21,589	384.93
Transport Equipments	49	276	463.26	8,649	16,815	94.41
Other Manufacturing Industries	53	167	215.09	3,708	4,550	22.71
Total	900	8,237	815.22	63,373	457,526	621.96

Source: Statistical Abstract of Haryana, 2000-01, pp. 382-92.

(b) Contribution of Constituents of Industrial Sector to Net Domestic Product of Haryana

The income generated by any sector is an important indicator of the performance of that sector. Thus, in order to look at the performance of the industrial sector, it is important to look for value-added by the industrial sector over a period. This will help us in studying the pattern of industrialisation. The secondary sector consists of three sub-sectors, namely, Manufacturing (registered and unregistered), Construction, Electricity, gas and water supply. The manufacturing sector is broadly classified into two sub-sectors, i.e. registered and unregistered. The share of registered sector in manufacturing shows the extent of development they have made in Haryana from 1966 to 2001. Unregistered units usually comprise of very small and repair oriented units. In order to have clear picture about Haryana's industrial growth, it is important to analyse the factor income generated by each sector since the inception of the state. The Table 6.8 shows sector-wise Net Domestic Product of the state from 1970-71 to 2001-02. The Table 6.8 shows that the contribution of electricity sector in Net Domestic Product was only Rs. 9.98 crores in 1970-71, which increased to Rs. 33.37 crores in 1980-81 and to Rs. 510.17 crores in 2001-02. In the manufacturing sector, though the steady growth was noticed in contribution of both registered and unregistered units over the period, but the registered units have shown the higher growth than unregistered units. The contribution of registered manufacturing units in Net Domestic Product has gone up from Rs. 58.45 crores in 1970-71 to Rs. 304.80 crores in 1980-81 and to Rs. 7,335.88 crores in 2001-02. The unregistered manufacturing units contributed Rs. 27.42 crores in 1970-71 and Rs. 2,925.88 crores in 2001-02. The construction sector contributed Rs. 36.41 crores to Net State Domestic Product in 1970-71. Its contribution rose to Rs. 3,586.58 crores in 2001-02. Thus, it follows that the secondary sector as a whole has witnessed a remarkable growth since the inception of Haryana state.

(c) Growth in the Industrial Production

Industrialisation is regarded as the key to economic

TABLE 6.8

Contribution of Secondary Sector to Net State Domestic Product (NSDP) (Current Prices)

Year	*Registered Manu-facturing*	*Un-registered Manu-facturing*	*Total Manu-facturing*	*Electricity, Gas and Water Supply*	*Construction*	*Total Contribution to NSDP*
1970-71	58.45	27.42	85.87	9.98	36.41	132.26
1980-81	304.8	123.84	428.64	33.37	113.14	575.15
1993-94	2,338.41	1,250.37	3,588.78	(-)136.72	1,479.25	4,931.31
1994-95	3,171.12	1,445.21	4,616.33	(-)26.03	1,708.39	6,298.69
1995-96	4,094.77	1,669.04	5,763.81	434.76	1,912.00	8,110.57
1996-97	4,581.91	1,890.85	6,472.76	427.99	2,120.59	9,021.34
1997-98	5,149.64	2,047.90	7,197.54	485.34	2,494.47	10,177.35
1998-99	5,634.52	2,314.45	7,948.97	264.72	2,860.86	11,074.55
1999-00	6,558.16	2,459.09	9,017.25	240.6	2,973.81	12,231.66
2000-01	7,137.53	2,644.23	9,781.76	527.38	3,179.31	13,488.45
2001-02	7,335.88	2,925.88	10,261.76	510.17	3,586.58	14,358.51
2002-03	9,119.27	3,044.51	12,163.78	643.26	3.680.11	16,487.15

Source: Statistical Abstract of Haryana, 2002-03, p. 201.

development of a country particularly in the field of production and employment. In the present days of planning, availability of reliable and up-to-date industrial statistics is an important pre-requisite for formulation and evaluation of industrial programmes. For this, index of industrial production is one of the most macro-economic indicator which reflects the change in the industrial scenario of the state over time. This index not only reflects the change in industrial sector but is also an important tool for measuring progress or decline in the concerned sectors of the Economic over time.

Economic and statistical organisation of Haryana calculates the index number of industrial production, which gives a clue to the industry-wise growth and general growth of industrial sector in the Economic. The index of industrial production is shown in Table 6.9.

TABLE 6.9

Index of Industrial Production in Haryana

Year	*Index (Base: 1970-71=100)*	*Index (Base: 1993-94=100)*
1981-82	250.51	—
1982-83	263.43	—
1983-84	280.84	—
1984-85	298.98	—
1985-86	334.55	—
1986-87	364.04	—
1987-88	396.44	—
1988-89	445.18	—
1989-90	461.67	—
1990-91	501.28	—
1991-92	531.5	—
1992-93	518.17	—
1993-94	—	100
1994-95	—	109.46
1999-00	—	161.17
2001-02	—	180.67

*Provisional.

Source: Economic Survey of Haryana, 2003-04, p. 106.

As shown in the Table 6.9, the index from 1981-82 to 1992-93 have been calculated on the basis of 1970-71 as base year, while from 1993-94 onward they have been calculated with 1993-94 as base year.

The Table 6.9 shows that the general index of industrial production with 1993-94 as base year (Revised Series) rose from 109.46 in 1994-95 to 161.57 in 1999-00 registering a growth of 52.11 per cent over 1994-95, it may be mentioned that the index of manufacturing sector rose from 151.74 in 1998-99 to 161.55 in 1999-00 exhibiting an increase of 6.47 per cent. The index of electricity sector has shown a significant increase from 119.82 in 1998-99 to 162.97 in 1999-00. The index of basic goods industries like gases, fertilizers, cement, etc. increased from 123.50 in 1998-99 to 130.73 in 1999-00 recording an increase of 5.85 per cent. The index of capital good industries like tractors, air conditioning plants, electric motors, etc. stood at 150.40 in 1999-00, while the index of intermediate goods stood at 149.88 and the index of consumer good industry stood at 177.39 in 1999-00.[11]

The general index of industrial production as well as industrial index industry-wise clearly reveal the remarkable increase over the base year, which indicates that Haryana is rapidly moving on the road of industrialisation.

V. LARGE AND MEDIUM SCALE INDUSTRY IN HARYANA

The large and medium scale industry deserves a detailed discussion because of its strong regional and local impact. It forms a special category amongst the registered factories. A large and medium scale unit is one, which is not only registered, but has an investment in plant and machinery of more than Rs. 1 crore in general and Rs. 5 crores in some specific industries.

In 1966, Haryana had 157 large and medium scale industries scattered over 24 places as shown in Table 6.10.

The Table shows that Faridabad with 83 units had biggest concentration of large and medium scale industries. Yamuna Nagar and Ballabhgarh ranked next with 10 units each. Jind district did not have even a single large and medium scale industry at that time.

It is important that after the formation of Haryana State, there has been striking growth in the number of large and medium industries as well as their distribution all over the state as demonstrated in Table 6.11.

Table 6.11 shows that in year 2000, there were 722 large and medium scale units scattered all over the state. However, Gurgaon and Faridabad with 226 and 175 units dominated the scene. These two districts are virtually extension of Delhi. Originally conceived as a rehabilitation project for displayed persons from Pakistan, these have grown into impressive industrial districts with projects like Maruti, Escorts, Good Year, Kelvinator, Godrej, etc.

Large and medium scale industry are dispersed to some villages also. This followed the declaration of

TABLE 6.10

Distribution of Large and Medium Scale Industry (1966)

District	*Industrial Centres*	*Number of Units*
Ambala	Ambala (6), Pinjore (1), Yamuna Nagar (10)	21
Bhiwani	Bhiwani (3), Dadri (1)	4
Faridabad	Ballabhgarh (10), Faridabad (83)	93
Gurgaon	Gurgaon (5)	5
Hisar	Hisar (5)	5
Jind	—	—
Karnal	Karnal (1), Panipat (3)	4
Kurukshetra	Shahbad (1)	1
Mahindragarh	Mandi Ateli (1), Rewari (1)	2
Rohtak	Bahadurgarh (6), Rohtak (3)	9
Sirsa	Sirsa (2)	2
Sonipat	Ganaur (1), Murthal (1), Narela (1), Sonipat (8)	11
Haryana		**157**

Source: Directory of Large and Medium .Scale Industries of Haryana.

Mahindragarh, Bhiwani, Hisar, parts of Ambala and Rohtak district as industrially backward for special assistance. Many industrialists located their enterprises in the villages of those districts, which enjoyed proximity to Delhi. Sonipat district is the example of this type of concentration. It has 90 units of large and medium scale industries.

VI. SMALL-SCALE INDUSTRIES IN HARYANA

Small-scale industry enjoys a special place in industrial development of Haryana, but before analyzing the growth of small-scale industry in the state it is necessary to define the concept of small-scale industry. Small-scale industry is defined differently in different countries. The concept of small-scale industry in few selected countries is given below:[12]

(A) Japan

In Japan, Small-scale industry is defined both in terms of employment and investment. Those units are called small-

TABLE 6.11

Number of Large and Medium Scale Industry in Haryana (2000)

District	*No. of Units*
Ambala	6
Bhiwani	9
Faridabad	175
Fatehabad	3
Gurgaon	226
Hisar	25
Jhajjar	36
Jind	13
Kaithal	1
Karnal	13
Kurukshetra	7
Mahindragarh	—
Panchkula	14
Panipat	33
Rewari	41
Rohtak	15
Sirsa	7
Sonipat	90
Yamuna Nagar	8
Total	**722**

Source: Directory of Large and Medium Scale Industries of Haryana (2000).

scale units, which have investment upto 100 million Yen or where not more than 300 workers are working.

(B) United States of America

In U.S.A those units are small-scale units, which employ not more than 100 workers.

(C) Korea

Those units are small-scale units, which employ

workers between 5 and 300 and have investment of 500 million WON.

(D) China

In China small-scale industry is defined in terms of production capacity in different industries. For example, in iron and steel industry units, those units are small-scale units, which have production capacity upto 10,000 tonnes. While in cement industry, units with production capacity upto 2,00,000 tonnes are included in small-scale sector.

Dhar and Lydall divided small-scale industries into three categories.[13]

(i) Cottage Industry

These are generally associated with agriculture and part time and whole time occupations in rural and semi-urban areas.

(ii) Agro-based Industries

These industries are based on processing of agricultural produce or they cater to input need of agriculturalists.

(iii) Small-scale Industries

These are divided into two parts:

(a) Modern Small-scale Manufacturing Enterprises

These are small firms using modern techniques to produce modern products. These firms, by their very nature are located in large towns in order to take advantage of external production economies. They use hired labour and raw material supplied by large-scale industries.

(b) Intermediate Group of Small Enterprises

These are those which use more or less traditional techniques to produce modern products. Here machine production is substituted by labour intensive non-mechanised (capital saving) techniques. The orientation of these enterprises is towards urban areas as they procure their raw material from towns, which also provide market for finished products.

Government of India has defined small-scale industries in its various industrial policy resolutions. These resolutions have divided small-scale industries into three sub-parts:

- Small-scale Enterprises,
- Small-scale ancillary units, and
- Tiny units.

Industrial policy statement of 1980 has defined small-scale enterprises as those enterprises with a fix capital investment of less than 20 lakhs and fixed capital investment of 25 lakhs in ancillary units. The investment limits for tiny units was 2 lakhs. In March 1985, the government revised the investment limit of small-scale to Rs. 35 lakhs and for ancillary units to Rs. 45 lakhs.

As per industrial policy statement of May 1990, the investment ceiling in plant and machinery for small-scale industry was revised from Rs. 35 lakhs to Rs. 60 lakhs and for ancillary units from Rs. 45 lakhs to 75 lakhs. The investment ceiling in respect of tiny units was increased form Rs. 2 lakhs to Rs. 5 lakhs. According to the modified definition an ancillary units is one, which sells not less than 50 per cent of its produce to one or more industrial units.

During 1997, on the recommendation of Abid Hussain committee, the government raised the investment limit on plant and machinery for small units and ancillary from 75 lakhs to Rs. 3 crores and for the tiny units from Rs. 5 lakhs to 25 lakhs. The government in 2000 has reduced the investment limit on plant and machinery from Rs. 3 crores to Rs. 1 crore but the limit for investment in tiny units has been retained at Rs. 25 lakhs.

Small-scale industries have made remarkable progress in Haryana. At the time of formation of Haryana State, i.e. in the year 1966 it had only 4,519 small-scale units. This number has jumped to 70,184 in 2000-01. The district-wise progress of small-scale undertakings in Haryana is shown in Table 6.12.

The Table 6.12 shows that at the time of formation of state Ambala district was the focal point of small-scale units having 38.8 per cent of total small sector units in the state. This share has declined to only 5.09 per cent in 2001. It is

TABLE 6.12

Small-Scale Units in Haryana

District	*No. of Units (1966)*	*% of Total*	*No. of Units (2001)*	*% of Total*
Ambala	1,752	38.8	3,578	5.09
Bhiwani	126	2.8	2,567	3.66
Faridabad	454	10	10,342	14.73
Gurgaon	368	8.1	8,341	11.88
Hisar	53	1.2	5,386	7.67
Karnal	584	12.9	4,034	5.75
Kurukshetra	215	4.8	2,784	3.97
Jind	200	4.4	2,913	4.15
Mahindragarh	—	—	2,312	3.29
Rohtak	333	7.4	3,253	4.63
Sonipat	327	7.2	5,432	7.74
Sirsa	30	0.7	3,299	4.7
Yamuna Nagar	—	—	5,124	7.3
Panipat	—	—	4,234	5.86
Kaithal	—	—	2,374	3.38
Rewari	—	—	2,388	3.4
Panchkula	—	—	1,534	2.19
Jhajjar	—	—	113	0.16
Fatehabad	—	—	176	0.25
Total	**4,519**	**100**	**70,184**	**100**

Source: Directorate of Industries, Haryana (Chandigarh).

due to division of the district into Yamuna Nagar and Panchkula district. At present Faridabad district occupies first place with 14.73 per cent of total units. Gurgaon, Sonipat, Hisar and Yamuna Nagar districts with only 11.88, 7.74, 7.67 and 7.30 per cent of total units respectively in the state follow it. The Table also reveals that Jhajjar and Fatehabad are least developed as far as small scale units are concerned with .16 and .25 per cent of total units respectively.

The analysis of above Table also reveals that small-scale industries are spread all over the state but the districts with proximity to Delhi still have greater concentration of small-scale units just as the case of large and medium scale units.

VII. PUBLIC SECTOR ENTERPRISES IN HARYANA

Public sector enterprises in Haryana are very limited in number. Existing public sector units in Haryana are as follows:

(1) Hindustan Machine Limited, Pinjore.
(2) National Fertilizers Limited, Panipat.
(3) Indian Pharmaceutical Limited, Dudaheda.
(4) Bharat Electronics Limited, Panchkula.
(5) Cement Corporation of India, Charkhi Dadri.
(6) Refinery of Indian Oil Corporation, Panipat.

The state enterprises are as follows:

(1) Haryana Breweries Limited, Murthal.
(2) Haryana Concost Limited, Hisar.
(3) Haryana Minerals Limited, Narnaul.
(4) Haryana Tanneries Limited, Jind.
(5) Haryana Agro Industries Corporation, Chandigarh.
(6) Haryana Dairy Development Corporation, Chandigarh.

VIII. EXPORT SCENARIO IN HARYANA

In export, Haryana has made tremendous improvement. In 1966, when Haryana came into being, its exports were only Rs. 4.5 crore per annum, which has increased to about Rs. 7000 crore in 2001. I.T. industry in Gurgaon alone is exporting software of about Rs. 3000 crore. After Karnataka and Andhra Pradesh, Haryana is the third largest exporter in software. Beside, other main items which are exported from Haryana are readymade garments, auto parts, cars, motor cycles, chemical, rice, guargum, handloom, carpet, scientific instruments, etc.[14]

IX. LOCATION OF INDUSTRY IN HARYANA

As far as location of industry in Haryana is concerned the growth is very lop-sided. Most of the industry (2/3) is concentrated in the districts, which have proximity to Delhi or have proximity to state capital Chandigarh. The reason for this lop sided growth is that industry always tend to locate itself in the region where it find ready market for its produce and raw material is easily available. Haryana government is aware of this lop sided growth; it has identified industrially backward areas in the state and with the help of HSIDC (Haryana State Industrial Development Corporation), it is setting up new industrial estates in the backward areas and is providing various facilities and incentives to industries in these areas.

X. ROLE OF HARYANA GOVERNMENT IN INDUSTRIAL DEVELOPMENT

From a relatively backward and pre-dominantly agricultural state at the time of its formation in 1966, Haryana has steadily risen to its pre-eminent position in the industrial sphere as well. This has been achieved largely because of number of favourable factors such as excellent law and order situation, an industrial relations climate conducive to industrial development, an extensive road and communication network, dedicated manpower and most importantly its geographical location with easy access to domestic consumer markets as well as exports outlets. All this make Haryana an ideal location for industry, but the most notable contribution in the industrial development of the state is the role of state government in making Haryana an excellent example of industrial development. The contribution of government of Haryana is manifested in its industrial policy statement of 1997. The policy is explained below:

(I) Objectives of Industrial Policy of 1997[15]

The policy objectives for industrial development are:

(a) Securing balanced industrial growth of the state with special emphasis on accelerating development of the relatively backward area of the state, so that there is economic and social justice for all.
(b) Creating new employment opportunities for the ever-increasing number of young unemployed.
(c) Strengthening and upgrading the existing infrastructure on priority basis with special emphasis on power and communication.
(d) Promoting new and consolidating the existing industries in the rural and small sector as also agro-based ones' so that vast majority of the state's population can readily find employment opportunities and state can fully utilize its agricultural produce.
(e) Providing an eco-friendly environment conducive to healthy growth of industries in the state.
(f) Channelising the flow of foreign investment and technology.

(2) Strategy of Industrial Policy of 1997

In the changed economic climate, Haryana's industrial policy needs to be radically different from what it has been to date. Dependency on government must give way to the new policy which seeks the co-operation and partnership of employees as well as the investors, both domestic as well as foreign. With this background the strategy of industrial policy of 1997, underlined the following steps:[16]

(a) Adopting a policy of infrastructure led growth and increasing private sector participation in infrastructure development.
(b) Simplifying procedures, eliminating red tapism and will-full delays and ensuring transparency in decision-making.
(c) Rationalising incentives, i.e. making them more effective and meaningful.
(d) Planning human resource development and improving the availability of skilled and semi-skilled manpower.

(e) Identifying the "thrust areas" in the specific industrial sectors in which Haryana enjoys advantage over other states and ensuring their optimal economic activity and quality control. Some of these industries are: (i) Electronics, (ii) Automobiles and Auto components, (iii) Handloom, Hosiery and Textiles, and (iv) Food and Agro-based industry.

The policy aims at increasing the annual industrial growth rate from 7.7 per cent to 12 per cent and increasing the present share of industries in State Domestic Product from around 24 per cent to 30 per cent.

With this strategy in view Haryana government has initiated a number of steps for industrial development of the state. Some of the steps are following:

- Industry-specific Infrastructure;
- Financial Infrastructure;
- Scheme of Incentives;
- Simplification of Rules and Procedures;
- Identifying Backward Areas; and
- Industry-specific Infrastructure.

The state government has formulated an industrial infrastructural development policy (IIDP), with a view to adopt an integrated approach to develop industrial infrastructure with a provision for increased participation of the private sector. Haryana State Industrial Development Corporation (HSIDC) has been earmarked as nodal agency for the development of industrial infrastructure of the state. This corporation is developing integrated industrial complexes throughout the state and towards this approach it is identifying new areas where the new industrial complexes can be set-up. It has also identified various areas in national capital region and other areas for development of industrial estates. The areas are following:[17]

(a) Industrial Estates in National Capital Region

HSIDC has identified six areas in national capital region,

where it is developing new industrial estates. These are:

(i) IMT, Manesar, on National Highway-8 (NH 8), where 1,736 acres land is acquired.
(ii) Growth Center, Bawal, which is 70 km from Delhi on NH 8. 1,200 acres of land is in the possession of HSIDC for development of industrial estate.
(iii) EPIP, Kundli, on NH 1, which is fully developed and allotments are being made for industries.
(iv) Kundli Phase-IV, located on NH 1, which is 55 km from Delhi, 500 acres of land acquired.
(v) Barhi, near Ganaur, on NH 1, which is around 40 km. from Delhi, 400 acres of land being acquired.
(vi) Palwal, located on NH 2, where 400 acres of land is being developed for industrial estates.

(b) Industrial Estates in Other Areas

Beside national capital region, the state is developing industrial estates in other areas also, some of these are:

(i) Growth Centre, Saha (Ambala), 400 acres of land is acquired.
(ii) Industrial Estate Barwala (Panchkula), is a fully developed industrial estate and allotments are being made to industrialists.
(iii) Industrial Estate, Manakpur (Yamuna Nagar), 120 acres of land is acquired.
(iv) IIDC, Bhiwani, where 64 acres of land is acquired.

Beside these industrial estates, the Haryana government is identifying new areas for setting of industrial estates. Some of the special features and facilities offered in these industrial estates are following:

- Industrial projects with investment of more than Rs. 50 crores are allotted plots in these industrial complexes immediately on receipt of request.
- Development of integrated industrial model township having infrastructural facilities of international standards are given high priority.

One such township is being developed at Manesar, district, Gurgaon.

- State is developing special technology parks to attract foreign as well domestic investment in setting of high tech projects. One such project is Singapore Technology Park at Gurgaon.
- Export promotion industrial parks are being developed to boost industrial exports from the state. One such park is set-up at Kundli (Sonipat).
- To provide self-employment opportunities to the rural youth, small industrial estates known as Udyog Kunj are being set-up in different parts of the state. Eight such Udyog Kunj have already developed and eight other are nearing completion.
- Under the new policy, the maintenance of industrial estates and upgradation facilities has been accorded highest priority.

Financial Infrastructure

Haryana Financial Corporation (HFC) and Haryana State Industrial Development Corporation (HSIDC) are the two state financial institutions engaged in providing financial assistance to the industrial units. These two corporations are providing following facilities:[18]

- Term lending
- Loan upto Rs. 150 lakhs per borrower
- Leasing
- Working Capital Loans
- Bill discounting
- Merchant banking
- Investment banking

Under the term lending activities HSIDC has so far sanctioned loan of Rs. 997.35 crores to 896 units. During the year 2000-01, HSIDC has sanctioned loan of Rs. 126.70 crores and disbursed Rs. 66.10 crores. Haryana Financial Corporation (HFC) has disbursed loan of Rs. 1,413 crores since its inception. In the year 2000-01 it has sanctioned loan of Rs. 98.99 crores. Besides these two corporations Haryana

Khadi and Village Industry Board is also providing loan for rural industry. It has disbursed loan of Rs. 1,021.39 lakhs in favour of 142 rural industries under the rural employment guarantee programme of Government of India.[19]

Scheme of Incentives

In order to attract investment in the state, special incentives in the form of sale tax exemption/deferment, exemption from payment of octroi, exemption from payment of electricity duty and special incentives to tiny and rural industries have been provided. The scheme of incentives may be summarised as follows:[20]

Scheme of Sales Tax Exemption/Deferment

The government of Haryana has divided state into three zones for the purpose of grant of sales tax exemption/ deferment as explained below:

- Zone 'A': Backward areas and IIDC, Bhiwani and Sirsa, Industrial Estate Jind, Karnal and Smalkha, Growth Centres at Saha and Bawal and Industrial Estate at Bahri, Palwal and Rozka-Meo.
- Zone 'B': New backward areas and Industrial Estates other than those mentioned in Zones 'A' and 'C'.
- Zone 'C': Areas falling in Faridabad and Ballabhgarh blocks of district Faridabad, Gurgaon block of district Gurgaon, Bahadurgarh block of district Rohtak, Rai block of district Sonipat, Udyog Vihar Phases I to VI Gurgaon, Electronic city, Hi-Tech Technology Park Gurgaon and Kundli Phases I and II.

The benefit of sales tax exemptions in these zones are as per scale given on next page.

Beside this, in the case of electronic industry, the benefit of sales tax exemption would be uniform for 7 years upto 300 per cent of fixed capital investment to the industrial unit set-up in Zones 'A' and 'B', while the benefit of sales tax deferment would be uniform for 7 years upto 300 per cent of fixed capital investment in Zones 'A', 'B' and 'C'.

Sales Tax Exemption

Zone	Small Scale	Medium Scale/ Large Scale	Time Limit
Zone 'A'	150% of Fixed Capital Investment	125% of Fixed Capital Investment	9 Years
Zone 'B'	125% of Fixed Capital Investment	100% of Fixed Capital Investment	7 Years
Zone 'C'	Not Applicable		

Sales Tax Deferment

Zone	Small Scale	Medium Scale/ Large Scale	Time Limit
Zone 'A'	175% of Fixed Capital Investment	150% of Fixed Capital Investment	9 Years
Zone 'B'	150% of Fixed Capital Investment	125% of Fixed Capital Investment	7 Years
Zone 'C'	125% of Fixed Capital Investment	100% of Fixed Capital Investment	5 Years

(b) Exemption from Payment of Electricity Duty

All new industrial units except those in the negative list of industries are exempted from payment of electricity duty for a period of 5 years throughout the state.

(c) Incentive to Tiny Units

The industrial units set-up under rural industry scheme as formulated in industrial policy 1997 are getting capital investment subsidy at the rate of 25 per cent of investment in fixed capital assets, subject to the ceiling of Rs. 2 lakhs. In addition these units are eligible for following benefits:[21]

- Electricity duty exemption, octroi and sales tax exemption/deferment at par with other units in small scale sector.
- Price preference of 10%.
- Marketing assistance.

(d) Incentives to the Trader and Business Community

The state government has given a number of incentives to the traders and business community due to the persistent demand of the people. In this context the tax structure has been rationalised. In place of all statutory forms like ST-14, ST-15, etc., the dealers are merely required to furnish a list of purchases and sales alongwith self printed certificates on the bills for claiming various concessions. The state government has introduced a new scheme of deemed assessment. Under this scheme all the cases of the turnover upto Rs. 5 crores are covered. The registered dealers shall not be required to submit any form (except forms prescribed under the C.S.T. Act) after submission of profit and loss and trading accounts in respect of their business. In case, on verification of the statement filed alongwith returns, no irregularity is detected, such cases shall be considered as deemed assessed. Whereas all previous cases would stand covered under the scheme. Further cases shall only be covered under the scheme in case there is increase in the sales tax receipt by 8 per cent as compared to the previous year's receipt. The necessity of furnishing the declaration alongwith last returns has been abolished under the Haryana General Sales Tax Act, 1973. In addition the tax has been reduced/exempted on the following items from 15/10/2001:[22]

(i)	Fertilizers	4% to 0%
ii)	Pesticide, Weedicide, Insecticide	4% to 2%
(iii)	Diesel	12% to 10%

(e) Uninterrupted Power Supply

In order to accelerate the process of economic development Haryana government had promised uninterrupted power supply upto one megawatt in 18 industrial estates. In these industrial estates all the existing units and new units will get uninterrupted power supply. These industrial estates are as follows:[23]

1. Roz-Ka-Meo
2. Hathen
3. Panchkula

4. Kurukshetra
5. Panipat
6. Kojka
7. Samalkha
8. Kundli
9. Rewari
10. Dharuhera
11. Jind
12. Bhiwani
13. Hisar
14. Tohana
15. Murthal
16. Sirsa
17. Bahadurgarh
18. Narnaul

(f) Quality Control

Haryana government is aware of the fact that in modern competitive world quality control is essential. Therefore, Haryana government has set-up 9 quality control centers in the state as per detail given below:

- Quality marking centers for Engineering goods at Jagadhri.
- Quality marking centers for Textile goods at Panipat.
- Quality marking centers for Engineering goods at Faridabad.
- Quality marking centers for Engineering and Chemical goods at Sonipat.
- Quality marking centers for Leather goods at Karnal.
- Quality marking centers for Electrical goods at Faridabad.
- Quality marking centers for Engineering goods at Hisar.
- Quality marking centers for Engineering goods at Bahadurgarh.
- Quality marking centers for Rubber and Engineering goods at Gurgaon.

(g) Negative List of Industries

Haryana government has identified 43 negative industries, which can not avail of above mentioned incentives:[24]

- Oil Expellers.
- Dal Mills and Rice Mills.
- Steel and Wooden Furniture.
- Stone Crusher.
- Power Cables except XLP Cables and fiber optic Cables.
- Paraffin wax based industries excluding Chlorinated paraffin wax and the industry where the paraffin wax is required in nominal quantity, i.e. only upto 5 per cent of the total raw material consumed by the unit.
- Corrugation of G.P./B.P. Sheets.
- Caustic soda units except those based on membrance cell technology.
- Simple fabricated items like trunks, buckets, gamlas, windows, grills and trusses, etc.
- Ethanol-based industries except non-molasses alcohol industries.
- Khandsari units.
- Bricks made of ordinary earth including mechanized bricks where the ordinary earth by contents is more than 50 per cent.
- Thinners.
- Induction and ARC furnace with more than 0.6 MT capacity.
- AAC/ACSR conductors.
- L.P. Gas cylinders.
- Non-graded C.I. Casting.
- Roller Flour Mills.
- Re-rolling of mild steel.
- Cotton Ginning & Pressing.
- All servicing units not providing service directly to the industry for production.
- Soft drinks.
- Asbestos products.

- Distillery/Breweries.
- Solvent extraction plants.
- Oil Refinery (edible and non-edible).
- Vegetable Ghee.
- Ice Plants.
- Cotton Spinning Mill.
- Fertilizer.
- Sugar.
- Cement.
- Fermentation and Distillery.
- Aluminum.
- Thermal Power.
- Sulphuric Acid.
- Tanneries.
- Copper Smelter.
- Zinc Smelter.
- Iron and Steel.
- Pulp and Paper.
- Dye and Dye Intermediates.
- Pesticides manufacturing and formulation.

Simplification of Rules and Procedures

In spite of embarking upon a programme of economic and structural reforms and introduction of an array of deregulatory measures, there are still many areas, which need improvement. Despite some efforts to simplify rules and regulations, we are still facing old archaic rules and regulations, which have become serious handicap in development of industries. Accordingly the state government has taken number of steps to simplify rules and procedures. Some of the steps are following:[25]

- The state has abolished all physical barriers to trade and commerce, like sales tax barriers, barriers against free movement of food grains, etc.
- Visits of inspectors to the industrial units have been reduced to bare minimum statutory requirements. Tiny units set-up in the rural areas are not subjected to any inspection.
- The renewal of licences under the factory act,

which was being done every year is now required only after 5 years.

- Self-regulation system is introduced in respect of units, which adopt pollution control measures/ norms as per the rules.
- No NOC is required for setting of an industry in the area falling outside the controlled areas.
- Controlled area plans of each district are prepared and published.
- Government has decided that no NOC shall be required to be obtained by industrial units except for 17 highly polluting industries identified by government of India and 19 polluting industries identified by Haryana Pollution Control Board.
- Regular interaction is held with the various industrial associations to discuss the problem, which hinder the smooth and successful operation in the industry.
- Industrial assistance group is recognised and strengthened to co-ordinate the activities of various departments, authorities and corporations connected with the development of industries so as to ensure expeditious clearance and better liaison.

Identifying the Backward Areas

For the balanced regional development of the state it is necessary that backward areas must be identified and efforts must be made to develop them. The state government has identified 79 blocks out of total 111 blocks as industrially backward areas of the state[26] as given in Table 6.13.

With the identification of these backward blocks Haryana government is making earnest efforts to bring them on the road of industrial development.

In brief, it is clear that industrially, Haryana was a distinctly less developed part of the former Punjab. Even within Haryana territory most of the industry was confined to few districts and that too only to some places within them. Formation of Haryana saw deliberate efforts on the part of state government to promote industry. This was done

TABLE 6.13

Industrially Backward Areas of Haryana State

Name of the District	*Name of the Block*
Ambala	Barara, Naraingarh, Ambala
Bhiwani	Badhra, Bhawani Khera, Dadri–I, Loharu, Siwani, Tosham
Faridabad	Hathin, Hodel, Palwal
Gurgaon	Farukh Nagar, Ferozepur Zhirka, Nagina, Pataudi, Punhana, Taoru
Hisar	Adampur, Agroha, Barwala, Bass, Bhattu–Kalan, Narnaund, Hansi, Fatehabad, Uklana
Jind	Alewa, Narwana, Pillukhera, Safidon, Uchana
Kaithal	Guhla, Pundri, Rajound
Karnal	Assandh, Indri, Nissing, Nilokheri
Kurukshetra	Ladwa, Shahbad, Thanesar
Mahindragarh	Ateli Nangal, Kanina, Mahendergarh, Narnaul, Nangal Chaudhary
Panchkula	Barwala, Morni, Raipur Rani, Pinjore
Panipat	Bapauli, Israna, Madlauda, Samalkha
Rewari	Khol, Nahar
Rohtak	Beri, Jhajjar, Kalanaur, Lakhan Majra, Matan – Hain, Sampla, Salawas
Sirsa	Baragudha, Dabwali, Ellenabad, Odhan, Rania
Sonipat	Gohana, Kathura, Kharkhoda, Gannaur, Mudlana
Yamuna Nagar	Bilaspur, Chhachhroli, Radaur, Sadhura

Source: Haryana's Industrial Policy, 1997.

through establishment of several new industrial estates and identification of industrially backward areas for special incentives and opening of industrial units in public sector. A special effort was made to take benefit of the state's proximity to Delhi. All these strategies have borne fruit and Haryana is emerging as one of the important industrial center of north India.

Conclusively, we may say that in view of its strategic location, excellent infrastructural facilities, rich industrial base, an entrepreneur-friendly industrial policy, a vast reservoir of skilled manpower, peaceful law and order situation, responsive administration and effective institutional support, Haryana is the ideal choice for launching an industrial venture. Haryana is a state that thinks big and marches on while keeping pace with forces of change. One is compelled to say that Haryana is ultimate choice for industries in India.

Notes and References

1. P.C. Mahalanobis: The approach of operational research to planning in India, p. 6.
2. A.O. Hirschman: The Strategy of Economic Development, p. 7.
3. Murray D. Bryce: Industrial Development, p. 5.
4. Saxena and Gupta: Organisation, Finance and Management of Industries in India (1995), p. 1.
5. Statistical Abstract of Punjab (1947-50).
6. *Ibid.*
7. Director, Public Relations, Haryana, प्रपफुल्लित हरियाणा (1995).
8. Bhattacharya, S.N., Industrial Potential Survey—Its Nature and Problems in Developing Economies, p. 1.
9. Kulkarni, M.R.: Industrial Development (New Delhi, National Book Trust, 1971), p. 27.
10. Economic Survey of Haryana, 2001-02.
11. *Ibid.*, p. 33.
12. Ram K. Vepa: Modern Small Industry in India (1988), p. 65.
13. P.N. Dhar and H.F. Lydall: The Role of Small Enterprise in Indian Economic Development (Delhi, 1962), p. 12.
14. Economic Survey of Haryana, 2001-2002, p. 29.
15. Haryana's Industrial Policy, 1997, p. 1.
16. *Ibid.*, p. 2.
17. *Ibid.*, p. 6.
18. *Ibid.*, p. 10.
19. Economic Survey of Haryana, 2001-02, pp. 30-31.
20. Haryana's Industrial Policy, 1997 p. 11.
21. *Ibid.*, p. 14.
22. Economic Survey of Haryana, 2001-02, p. 34.
23. Haryana for Industry (1996), p. 18.
24. Haryana's Industrial Policy, 1997, pp. 18-20.
25. Haryana's Industrial Policy, 1997, p. 17.
26. *Ibid.*, pp. 18-19.

7

INFRASTRUCTURE FACILITIES IN HARYANA

The prosperity of a country depends directly upon the development of agriculture and industry. Agricultural production however, requires power, credit, transport facilities, etc. Industrial production requires not only machinery and equipment but also skilled manpower, management, energy, banking and insurance facilities, transport services, which include railways, roads and air transport, communication facilities, etc. All these facilities and services constitute collectively the infrastructure of an Economy. M.S. Patwardhan defined infrastructure "as comprising those basic services without which productive activities cannot take place. It includes all basic services from public health to education, transport and communication, irrigation and power, banking and finance, etc."[1]

Dr. S.M. Shah (1980) advocates a much broader concept in his 'Village Registers Scheme' for Indonesia. He conducted a survey of village facilities in Indonesia after every three years. It provided a comprehensive coverage of the infrastructural services essential for the growth of a rural Economic. The concept of infrastructure Implied in it include following types of infrastructural facilities:[2]

(i) Health services
(ii) Education
(iii) Communication
(iv) Social and Cultural Facilities
(v) Power and Water
(vi) Economic and Financial Services
(vii) Transportation Network

Though the concept of infrastructure proposed by Shah is meant for rural Economy, it is broad enough to meet the requirements of growth and development for industries and other sectors of the Economic.

Dr. V.K.R.V. Rao, in his key paper on the theme has also given a very comprehensive concept of infrastructure. He includes the following in his concept of infrastructure:[3]

(i) Transport;
(ii) Communication;
(iii) Energy;
(iv) Intermediate Goods Output (Mines and Minerals)
(v) Increasing the Productivity of Natural Resources such as Land, Animal Husbandry, Forestry and Fisheries;
(vi) Science and Technology;
(vii) Information System;
(viii) Financial System; and
(ix) Human Resource Development.

In short, infrastructural facilities can be summarised as under:

(i) *Energy*: Conventional and Non-conventional Sources.
(ii) *Transport*: Railways, Road, Shipping and Civil aviation.
(iii) *Communication*: Post & Telegram, Telephones, Telecommunication.
(iv) Banking, Finance and Insurance.
(v) Science and Technology.
(vi) *Social Overheads*: Health and Hygiene, Education, etc.

I. INFRASTRUCTURE AND ECONOMIC DEVELOPMENT

Economic development requires investment in both industry and agriculture. But a large amount of investment in infrastructure is also of equal importance. The traditional approach of allocating a major part of the resources to certain modern projects, which promise to be import savers and export generators, has not resulted in desirable changes in economic system. It is now increasingly realized by progressive economists and planners that to promote substantial economic growth, a large amount of investment is necessary for creating and developing the infrastructure of the country as a whole as well as in different regions of the country. The availability of infrastructure facilities stimulates more economic growth in agriculture and industry. The absence of adequate infrastructure facilities adversely affects the growth of agriculture and industries. The essential pre-requisites for agricultural development are adequate provision of water for irrigation, adequate and effective delivery system for modern farm inputs, development of regulated markets, agricultural credit and education, training and research in the field of agriculture. All these constitute infrastructure for agricultural development. In short, infrastructure is a necessary pre-condition for the development of the Economy of a country. In the words of Dr. V.K.R.V. Rao, "The link between infrastructure and development is not once for all affair. It is a continuous process; and progress in development has to be preceded, accompanied and followed by progress in infrastructure, if we are to fulfil our declared objectives of a self-accelerated process of economic development."[4]

II. INFRASTRUCTURAL FACILITIES IN HARYANA

In the present chapter an attempt is being made to analyse the growth of infrastructural facilities in Haryana, which have a close bearing on its economic development. The infrastructure facilities discussed in this chapter are:

(1) Energy

(2) Transport
(3) Communication
(4) Banking
(5) Tourism Infrastructure
(6) Infrastructure for Information Technology
(7) Education
(8) Health

(I) Energy

Energy, in one form or the other, is the most important input for any development and directly determines the pace of economic growth in any society. Haryana State has limited availability of natural resources of energy. There is no hydro-generation potential in the state. Even the coal-mines are far away located from the state. There is very limited forest area. Wind velocity prevailing in the state is also not sufficient to exploit for power generation. Although the solar intensity is relatively higher but the land area limitation does not encourage big scale harnessing of this resource as well. Therefore, the state has been depending on limited thermal generation capacity installed within the state and the hydropower from the jointly owned projects. The State's efforts have been supplemented by central generation projects from where the state gets share on the formula evolved by the Government of India for such projects.

The sources of energy in Haryana can be studied in two parts:

(a) Conventional Sources of Energy, and
(b) Non-conventional Sources of Energy.

(a) Conventional Sources of Energy

Conventional sources of energy consist of hydro, thermal and gas based sources of energy. The growth of conventional sources of energy in Haryana is discussed in Table 7.1. The Table shows that installed generation capacity of power in Haryana has risen from 29 MW in 1967-68 to 1,780 MW in 2000-01. Out of this total generation capacity 902 MW is hydel while 877.50 is thermal. Another note-worthy point is that the thermal source of energy has

TABLE 7.1

Installed Generation Capacity and Power Availability in Haryana

Year	Installed Generation Capacity (in M.W.)				Power Availability (Million K.W.H.)						Power Sold in Million (KWH)	Trans-mission and distribution losses (in million KWH)
	Hydel	Thermal	Internal Combustion Plant	Total	Hydel	Thermal	Total	Auxiliary Consumption	Power Purchased	Power Available		
1967-68	—	24.20	5.22	29.42	—	21.00	21.00	3.00	583.00	601.00	501.00	100.00
1970-71	—	24.20	5.22	29.42	912.00	298.00	1,210.00	8.00	44.00	1,246.00	903.00	343.00
1980-81	654.00	417.00	2.50	1,074.00	2,667.00	1302.00	4,269.00	205.00	120.00	4,184.00	3,391.00	793.00
1990-91	879.00	877.00	—	1,756.50	4,093.00	2445.00	3,738.00	327.00	2,614.00	9,025.00	6,641.00	2,384.00
2000-01	902.00	877.50	—	1,779.50	2,985.32	215.67	3,200.99	—	13,654.43	16,855.42	15,712.39	1,143.03
2001-02	917.00	1087.50	—	2,004.50	2,840.13	198.29	3,038.42	—	14,808.80	17,247.22	16,566.85	1,280.37

Source: Statistical Abstract of Haryana, 2001-02, pp. 448-49.

remained more or less constant since 1989-90 (877.50 MW) while hydro source has shown very less increase in the last decade. The power availability scenario depicted in the Table indicates that hydel and thermal sources constitute the main sources of energy and Haryana government is getting major part of its power from central resources like N.H.P.C. N.T.P.C., etc. The Table also shows that transmission and distribution losses in Haryana stood at 1,280.37 K.W.H. in 2001-02, which is almost 7% of the total power available. Haryana Vidyut Prasaran Nigam is making an earnest effort to reduce these transmission losses and it is due to these efforts that transmission losses, which were 4,745.64 K.W.H. in 1998-99, have come down to 1,280.37 K.W.H. in 2000-01.

After analyzing the installed generation capacity and power availability in Haryana it is necessary to analyse the infrastructure for distribution of the power in the state. This infrastructure is depicted in Table 7.2.

TABLE 7.2

L.T. and 11 KV Lines in Haryana (2001)

(Circuit Kilometer)

Districts	*L.T. Lines*	*11 KV Lines*	*No. of Transformers*
Hisar	8,465	6,154	9,536
Sirsa	4,965	2,960	7,116
Bhiwani	5,270	5,289	8,086
Gurgaon	8,434	3,283	5,807
Faridabad	7,283	3,128	6,167
Jind	5,261	3,352	5,393
Mahindragarh	13,543	5,560	9,601
Ambala	4,081	2,323	6,375
Karnal	16,834	6,808	17,645
Kurukshetra	13,920	7,003	18,356
Rohtak	5,562	3,113	4,164
Sonipat	4,282	2,999	4,809
Yamuna Nagar	7,456	3,635	7,800
Haryana	**1,05,356**	**55,607**	**1,10,855**

Note: The information for all the 19 districts is not available with HVPN.

Source: Haryana Vidyut Prasaran Nigam Limited, Statistical Abstract of Haryana, p. 431.

The Table shows the distribution network through L.T. lines, 11 KV lines and number of transformers. The Table shows that in 2001 total of L.T. lines in Haryana are 1,05,356 KM while that of 11 KV lines are 55,607 kilometers. This is remarkable improvement over the year 1967 when total L.T. lines in Haryana were just 9,796 kilometers and 11 KV lines were just 7,089 kilometers.[5] The study of various districts shows that the distribution of power through L.T. lines is more in comparison to 11 KV lines.

The discussion of power distribution in the state is incomplete without discussing the consumption of electricity scenario in the state. The purpose-wise percentage consumption of electricity is shown in the Table 7.3.

TABLE 7.3

Percentage Consumption of Electricity—Purpose-wise

Year	*Domestic*	*Industrial*	*Agricultural*	*Others*	*Total*
1966-67	6.8	62	22.7	8.5	100
1970-71	6.4	52.9	33.1	7.6	100
1980-81	8.9	47.7	37.3	6.1	100
1990-91	18.8	28.8	44.8	7.6	100
1994-95	19.8	24.1	46.7	9.4	100
2000-01	21.2	20.5	46.9	11.4	100
2001-02	21.54	23.22	43.57	11.67	100
2002-03	20.19	23.76	42.93	13.12	100

Source: H.V.P.N., Statistical Abstract of Haryana (2002-03), p. 442.

The Table shows that in 1966-67, i.e. at the time of inception of the state the industrial consumption of electricity was 62 per cent of the total, while agricultural consumption was only 22.7 per cent. But the picture is different in 2001-02, where agriculture is the largest consumer of electricity with 43.57 per cent of the total while the industrial use has declined to 23.22 per cent. This shows the rural bias of electricity consumption in Haryana. The total number of electricity consumers in the state is also rapidly increasing. It is 35.47 lakhs on March 2001. Every year nearly 1.5 lakh electricity connections are released.[6]

The per capita consumption of electricity is also increased over the time period as shown in Table 7.4.

TABLE 7.4

Unit Sold and Per Capita Consumption of Electricity

Years	*Units Sold (Lakh K.W.H.)*	*Units Sold Per Capita*
1966-67	4,343.32	48
1970-71	9,038.71	92
1980-81	25,557.18	206
1990-91	60,513.75	371
1995-96	83,522.33	454
2000-01	1,01,436.16	507
2001-02	1,06,074.47	522
2002-03	1,17,206.95	530

Source: H.V.P.N., Statistical Abstract of Haryana (2002-03), p. 446.

The Table shows that per-capita consumption of electricity, which was only 48 units in 1966-67, has increased to 522 units in 2001-02. This signifies improved power availability in the state.

Haryana State has two thermal power stations, one at Panipat and the other at Faridabad. Panipat thermal project has 4 units with the capacity of 110 M.W. each. The Faridabad thermal power project is installed with the help of N.T.P.C. and have a capacity of 432 M.W. A super thermal power project is proposed to be setup at Yamuna Nagar.

(b) Non-conventional Source of Energy

Non-Conventional source of energy consists of Solar energy, Nuclear energy, etc. Haryana has no nuclear source of energy and solar energy is the only non-conventional source of energy. The department of Non-Conventional energy sources is responsible for formulating policies and programmes necessary for popularizing the application of various non-conventional and renewable sources of energy in the state. It is implementing various schemes concerning utilisation of solar energy, biogas, micro-hydel, biomass energy, etc.

A solar thermal energy programme, which aims at providing solar energy alternative for thermal energy requirements is generating good response in the state. The state has about 300 sunny days and therefore, people have started utilizing solar energy for water heating applications in large numbers. During 2000-01, 11 systems with cumulative capacity of 2800 Lpd. were installed in the state. In order to increase the penetration of solar thermal technologies in industrial sector, particularly for textile units of Panipat, a concept paper was submitted to UNDP-GEF for its support.

Solar Photovoltaic System to supplement the electrical energy requirements are being promoted in the state. During the year 2000-01, 500 lanterns, 3,500 SPV domestic lighting systems, and 200 solar water-pumping systems[7] were installed. For the year 2001-02, the target is to install 6,000 solar lanterns, 4,250 SPV domestic lighting systems, 300 SPV street lighting systems and 50 solar water-pumping systems.

Under integrated rural energy programme (IREP), various types of renewable energy and energy efficient systems like solar cookers, improved kerosene stoves, solar lanterns, pressure cookers, solar-water heating systems, compact fluorescent lamps, SPV home lighting systems, SPV domestic lighting systems, SPV water pumping system, SPV stand alone street lighting system, etc. are being promoted through financial incentives. Demonstration and extension activities are being carried out in the IREP blocks for helping rural people to meet their cooking, heating and lighting energy needs by adopting these systems. During the year 2000-01, this programme was implemented in 39 blocks in the states and in the year 2001-02, 29,897 families are being covered. There is a proposal to extend this programme to 5 new blocks in the year 2001-02.

(2) Transport

If agriculture and industry are regarded as the body and bones of the economy, transport constitutes its nerves, which helps the circulation of men and materials. The transport system helps to broaden the market for goods, and by doing so, it makes possible large-scale production through division of labour. It is also essential for the movement of labour force, raw materials, fuels, machines, etc. to the places of production. Infact, "Transportation is vitally inter-linked with the economic development of the country. It allows land to be exploited economically, it leads industry and agro-industry to develop, it enables trade and commerce to proliferate and it motivates labours and capital to discover new frontiers."[8]

Wilfred Owen analyses the importance of transportation in economic development through a mobility index which combines available data on transport facilities and movement of passengers and freight. He states that immobility and poverty go together. The countries with low per capital GNP had a mobility index for freight and passenger transport in single digits, whereas this index was significantly high in countries with high per capita income.[9] Thus, we can say that growth and transportation goes together.

The study of transport facilities in Haryana can be divided into three parts:

(a) Road Transport
(b) Railways
(c) Air Transport

(a) Road Transport

The road transport in Haryana can be studied in two parts:

- Roads
- Road transport

I. Roads

Roads are basic means of communication for the development of any economy. A well-planned and efficient network of roads gives big boost to the process of economic development. It was emphasized in Seventh Five Year Plan that "........ since the country's economy is still largely agrarian in character and the settlement pattern is rural-oriented, roads constitute a critical element of transportation service."[10] Haryana state has an efficient network of roads, which is significantly contributing to its economic development. The total road length in Haryana is depicted in Table 7.5.

TABLE 7.5

Length of Metalled Roads in Haryana (2001)

(Kilometers)

District	*Total Length*	*Per 100 Sq. km. of area*	*Per lakh of Population*
Ambala	1,093	69.44	108
Panchkula	560	62.36	119
Yamuna Nagar	1,083	61.26	110
Kurukshetra	1,008	66.88	122
Kaithal	1,255	54.16	133
Karnal	1,101	43.38	86
Panipat	1,042	82.18	108
Sonipat	1,041	49.06	81
Rohtak	948	54.33	101
Jhajjar	885	48.26	100
Faridabad	1,209	56.21	55
Gurgaon	1,696	61.32	102
Rewari	984	62.20	129
Mahindragarh	945	50.83	116
Bhiwani	1,985	41.54	139
Jind	1,149	42.52	97
Hisar	1,851	46.47	120
Fatehabad	1,462	58.02	181
Sirsa	1,663	38.88	150
Haryana	22,960	51.93	109

Source: Engineer-in-Chief, Public Works Department (Building and Roads), Haryana, Statistical Abstract of Haryana (2000-01), p. 465.

The Table 7.5 shows that the total length of metalled roads in Haryana is 22,960 km. The road length per 100 sq.

km. of area is 51.93 km. while road length per lakh of population for the state is 109 km. The district-wise study of metalled roads shows that out of 19 districts in the states 11 districts have above state average metalled road length per 100 sq. km. of area, while 8 districts have below state average metalled road length. Sirsa district is having lowest road length, i.e. 38.88 km per 100 sq. km. of area.

Almost all the villages in the state are connected with metalled roads as is clear from the Table 7.6. Table 7.6 shows that in all the districts of the state almost all the villages are connected with metalled roads. The percentage of villages connected in Panipat, Mahindragarh and Jind is 100 per cent, while all other districts have above 95 per cent of villages connected with metalled roads.

TABLE 7.6

Percentage of Villages Connected with Metalled Roads

District	*1980-81*	*1990-91*	*2000-01*
Ambala & Panchkula	94.26	97.31	97.31
Yamuna Nagar	—	98.89	98.89
Kurukshetra	99.58	99.75	99.75
Kaithal	—	99.31	99.31
Karnal	96.47	99.20	99.20
Panipat	—	100.00	100.00
Sonipat	99.11	99.19	99.70
Rohtak and Jhajjar	99.30	99.58	99.58
Faridabad	92.30	96.71	96.71
Gurgaon	96.27	98.37	98.37
Rewari	—	99.75	99.75
Mahindragarh	99.15	100.00	100.00
Bhiwani	99.53	99.76	99.76
Jind	100.00	100.00	100.00
Hisar and Fatehabad	98.80	99.80	99.80
Sirsa	97.79	98.74	98.74
Haryana	97.31	98.99	98.99

Source: Economic and Statistical Organisation, Haryana, Statistical Abstract of Haryana, 2000-01, p. 467.

The Government of Haryana realises the importance of Roads in Economic development. The main emphasis of the Government is on the improvement/upgradation of roads network, construction of bye passes, bridges/ROB and completion of road construction work which are already in progress to further strengthen the road network and making it more efficient as per traffic requirements.

During the year 2001-02, a programme for repair of roads and filling pot holes in addition to widening, strengthening, reconstructing, raising cement concrete pavement in village portions and making drains/culverts was taken in hand on war footing. The progress achieved during the year 2001-02 is:[11]

Sr. No.	*Particulars*	*Unit in K.Ms.*
(i)	Repair with patch work and pot holes.	8140
(ii)	Improvement with widening/strengthening/reconstruction and raising, etc.	1260
(iii)	Premix carpet work.	2830
(iv)	Cement concrete pavement/block in village portion	28
(v)	Side drain	3
(vi)	Construction of new roads	24

Source: Economic Survey of Haryana, 2001-02, p. 35.

Haryana state has been striving very hard to improve and upgrade the road network and so has arranged sanction of projects amounting to Rs. 783.46 crores from HUDCO.

State Government has further processed proposals for raising loans from National Capital Region Planning Board for improvement of roads in National Capital region for an estimated cost of Rs. 65.00 crore and for construction of bridge under NABARD loan for estimated cost of Rs. 35 crore.[12]

Even in case of National Highways, four lanning of NH-1 from Karnal to Ambala Cantt and further to state border with the Punjab has been completed and land mark elevated highway at Ambala Cantt. and grade separator near tourist complex King Fisher, Ambala City has been completed and opened to traffic.

(a) Road Transport

A well planned and efficient network of transport is an essential component for a developing Economy. Adequate transport facilities are a pre-requisite to the all round development of the state. The Transport Department, Haryana is committed to provide adequate, well co-ordinated, economical and efficient bus services to the people of the state. Haryana Roadways has earned the reputation of being one of the best State Road Transport undertakings in the Country in the field of operational efficiency, staff productivity, lowest operational cost (without incidence of taxes) per effective KM operated and surplus before taxes, etc. It has continuously been striving to provide improved bus services and passenger amenities to the travelling public. The performance of State Road Transport Department can be analysed from Table 7.7.

TABLE 7.7

Performance of State Transport Department

Sl. No.	*Particulars*	*Unit*	*2001-02*	*2002-03*
1.	Buses held last day	No.	3493	3403
2.	Depot/Workshop	No.	20	20
3.	Sub-Depot/Workshop	No.	17	17
4.	Bus Stands	No.	82	82
5.	No. of Routes	No.	1634	1672
6.	Effective KMs	Lakh kms	2874.49	2992.35
7.	KMs operated/day	Lakh kms.	10.45	10.88
8.	Daily Passengers	Lakhs	10.74	11.13
9.	Number of Employees	No.	19176	19136
10.	Net Profit	Rs. Lakh	(-)3993.09	(-)5248.12
11.	Profit before tax	Rs. Lakh	6727.29	12085.20
12.	Resources contributed to State Exchequer	Rs. Crore	87.7	96.53

Source: Economic Survey of Haryana, 2003-04, p. 49.

The Table 7.7 shows that at present Haryana Roadways has 3403 buses being run from 20 main depots and 17 Sub-depots. These services cover about 10.88 lac kms. every day and carry about 11.13 lakh passengers daily. The state Transport Department has also constructed 82 modern bus stands at important places in the state. Apart from this, two central workshops have been set-up at Karnal and Hisar and a Drivers Training Institute has been set-up at Murthal. Facilities for training and certifying new heavy vehicle drivers have also been provided apart from Murthal at four centres, i.e. at Karnal, Hisar, Gurgaon and Rohtak.[13]

The Haryana Roadways is contributing a large amount to the State Exchequer. The contribution of Haryana Roadways to the State Exchequer is about 87 crores in 2001-02. The profit before tax during 2001-02 of Haryana Roadways is Rs. 65.80 crores which is the highest in the country.

With a view to ensure safety of passengers, to reduce accidents and for managing the traffic on modern lines on the important National Highways, an institution of Haryana Highways Patrol and Road Safety has been created in the Transport Department under SSP (HHP and RS), Karnal. 19 Traffic Aid Centres (TACs) at nearly every 30 Kms on NH 1, 2, 8 and 10 have been set-up. Each Traffic Aid Centre has been equipped with a patrol gypsy, motor cycle, a recovery crane and ambulance with para-medical staff. They have also been provided mobile phones, speed radars and also meters for effective checking against vehicles violating road safety norms. The TACs also keep in constant touch with the nearest Trauma care centres so that accident victims could be immediately shifted to these hospitals to save the precious lives. As per the data with SSP (HPP & RS), with the setting of TACs, the accidents on these National Highways during April-December, 2001 have come down by 15 per cent compared to the corresponding period last year.[14]

(b) Rail Transport

As far as rail transport is concerned, Haryana is well connected with different parts of the country. Delhi-Agra, Ajmer-Ferozepur, Delhi-Jammu railway lines cross through the state. Ambala, Panipat, Kurukshetra are the main railway stations in the state. There is also one railway workshop in Yamuna Nagar. The main rail routes passing through the state are:[15]

(i) Ambala-Delhi
ii) Kalka-Hawra
(iii) Rewari-Ahmedabad
(iv) Delhi-Ferozepur
(v) Amritsar-Howrah
(vi) Bhiwani-Rohtak-Delhi
(vii) Kalka-Jodhpur
(viii) Delhi-Shimla

(c) Air Transport

Haryana has one airport which is situated in state capital Chandigarh. Beside this there are five flying clubs at Hisar, Karnal, Pinjore, Narnoul and Bhiwani. Two major air bases of Indian air force are situated at Ambala and Hisar.

Haryana cannot boast of an efficient network of air transport but since it is situated near capital Delhi, it enjoys all the benefits of International Airport situated in Delhi.

3. Communication Infrastructure in Haryana

The communication infrastructure comprises post and telegraphs, telecommunication system, broadcasting, television and information system. By providing necessary information about the markets and also supplying necessary motivation, the communication system helps to bring buyers and sellers together effectively and helps to accelerate the growth of the Economy. Accordingly the modern communication system has become an integral part of the development process. The development of communication facilities in Haryana is shown in Table 7.8.

The Table shows a tremendous increase in communication facilities in the state. The number of post offices that were just 1,794 in 1966-67, has increased to 2,650. Similarly, number of telegraph offices and telephone exchanges has increased from 167 and 61 in 1966-67 to 394 and 965 respectively in 2001-02. The number of telephone connections stood at 9,88,109 in 2001-02.

TABLE 7.8

Communication Facilities in Haryana

Particulars	*1966-67*	*1970-71*	*1980-81*	*1990-91*	*2000-01*	*2001-02*
Post Offices	1,794	1,956	2,367	2,588	2,653	2,650
Telegraph Offices	167	198	780	392	394	394
Telephone Exchanges	61	92	134	411	905	965
Public Call Office	—	268	529	785	15,740	20,420
Telephone Connections	—	—	30,000	1,10,000	7,94,194	9,88,109

Source: Statistical Abstract of Haryana, 2001-02, p. 672.

4. Banking and Financial Institutions

Institutional finance is essential for any development programme. In Haryana, the role of the Government has been to persuade the Banking Institutions to give greater importance to the agricultural and allied sectors, particularly to poverty alleviation programmes. The institutional finance available through commercial, cooperative banks and other term lending institutions reduce pressure on the budgetary resources of the state Government.

The Banking development in the state is shown in the Table 7.9.

TABLE 7.9

Growth of Financial Institutions in Haryana

Type of Banks	*1966-67*	*1980-81*	*1990-91*	*2000-01*	*2001-02*
Indian Commercial Banks	122	779	1,260	1,508	1,549
Indian Scheduled Banks	121	778	1,260	1,508	1,549
Indian Non-Scheduled Banks	1	1	—	—	—
Foreign Banks	—	—	—	—	—
Co-operative Banks	36	196	263	344	348
Post Office Saving Banks	969	2,367	2,522	2,653	2,650
Total	1,127	3,342	4,045	4,505	4,547

Source: Reserve Bank of India Bulletin and Post Master General, Haryana Circle, Ambala, Statistical Abstract of Haryana, 2001-02, p. 537.

The Table 7.9 shows that in the year 2001-02 Haryana State had 1549 Indian Commercial Banks, 348 Cooperative Banks and 2650 Post Office Saving Banks. The total deposits of Commercial banks working in the state stood at Rs. 19,289 crore while the total advances of these banks in Haryana was Rs. 8,329 crores on 31st March 2001.

Scheduled Commercial banks are also advancing direct loans to agriculture sector. Amount of these advances (outstanding) as on 31st March, 2001 was Rs. 1,917 crore. Under the priority sector, Haryana State Co-operative Agriculture and Rural Development Bank has advanced Rs. 280.34 crore against the target of Rs. 348.64 crore for the year 2000-01 which is 80% of the annual target.[16]

The sector-wise performance of Haryana State Co-operative Agriculture and Rural Development Bank during the year 2000-01 is shown in Table 7.10.

TABLE 7.10

Advances by Haryana State Co-operative Agriculture and Rural Development Bank During 2000-01

(Rs. in crores)

Sector	*Targets*	*Achievements*	*Percentage*
Agriculture	315.54 (90.51)	262.42 (93.61)	83.2
Small Scale Industries	25.12 (7.20)	16.31 (5.82)	65.0
Tertiary	7.98 (2.29)	1.61 (0.57)	20.2
Total	348.64 (100.00)	280.34 (100.00)	80.4

Source: Economic Survey of Haryana, 2001-02, p. 62.

Credit Plan

Overall achievement for State Annual Credit Plan 2000-01 stood at Rs. 5431.41 crore against the annual target of Rs. 5259.06 crore which is 103.3 per cent of the annual target as compared to the achievement of 101.7 per cent registered during the corresponding period of the last year. Sector-wise details is shown in Table 7.11.

TABLE 7.11

Annual Credit Plan of Haryana for 2000-01

(Rs. in crores)

Sector	*Targets*	*Achievements*	*Percentage*
Agriculture	3577.82 (68.03)	3754.00 (69.12)	104.9
Small Scale Industries	1075.99(20.46)	1070.54 (19.71)	99.5
Tertiary	605.25 (11.51)	606.87 (11.17)	100.3
Total	5259.06(100.00)	5431.41(100.00)	103.3

Source: Economic Survey of Haryana, 2001-02, p. 62.

The performance under agriculture sector has also quite satisfactory. Against the target of Rs. 3577.82 crore, the achievement during the financial year 2000-01 was Rs. 3754.00 crore, i.e. 104.9% which is higher as compared to last year's achievement of 103.9 per cent.

In the Small Scale Industries sector, banks disbursed Rs. 1070.54 crore though the target was of Rs. 1075.99 crore, which was 99.5 per cent as compared to achievement of 92.9 per cent registered during the corresponding period of last year.

The achievement under Annual Credit Plan, 2000-01 in the Tertiary Sector has declined to 100.3 per cent as compared to 107.0 per cent during the corresponding period of last year. This slightly low performance was off-set by increased lending under this sector, i.e. Rs. 606.87 crore during 2000-01 as compared to Rs. 512.36 crore during the previous year.

The Haryana Co-operative Apex Bank Ltd. is providing credit facilities throughout the State through the existing 2406 Mini Banks (as on 31-3-2001). These Mini Banks are financially assisted by 17 Central banks functioning at the district level. The Haryana Co-operative Apex Bank Ltd. provides adequate credit facilities by securing the financial assistance from NABARD and also by involving its own resources. As on 31-3-2001 assistance to the tune of

Rs. 2146.81 crore was provided by the Haryana Co-operative Apex Bank Ltd. at the State level.[17]

The discussion on financial institutions in Haryana is incomplete without discussing the role of Haryana State Industrial Development Corporation (HSIDC) and Haryana Financial Corporation (HFC).

The Haryana State Industrial Development Corporation (HSIDC) was established in March 1967, under the guidelines issued by the Government of India. The corporation has been playing the role of an institutional entrepreneur as well as development-cum-financial institution for accelerating the pace of industrial growth in the state, primarily in the medium and large scale sector. The activities of the Corporation are grouped under following heads:

I. To provide industrial infrastructure in the State of Haryana.
II. To provide term loan assistance to industrial units as a state level financial institution.
III Providing merchant banking services to industries.
IV. To set-up industrial units in the public/joint assisted sectors.

With the support of the state government HSIDC has shown an all-round growth in its performance over the last five years. The operation of the corporation has not only been profitable but has also been diversified taking full benefits of the new policies of the Government. HSIDC has so far sanctioned loan of Rs. 997.25 crores to 896 units. During the year 2000-01, it has sanctioned loan of Rs. 126.70 crore and disbursed Rs. 66.10 crore. In the year 2001-02, HSIDC has sanctioned loan of Rs. 56.67 crore and disbursed Rs. 34.73 crore.[18]

Haryana Financial Corporation (HFC) has been set-up under an Act of Parliament known as State Financial Corporation's Act, 1951 and the working is governed by this Act. HFC meets the credit needs of small and medium scale industrial units by advancing term loan. The loans are advanced primarily for acquiring fixed assets such as land, building, plant and machinery. Haryana Financial

Corporation (HFC) in the year 2001-2002 (upto December, 2001), sanctioned loan of Rs. 98.99 crore and disbursed loan Rs. 41.74 crore and since its inception it has sanctioned loan of Rs. 2250.89 crore and disbursed loan of Rs. 1413 crore.[19]

6. Tourism Infrastructure

A vast tourist infrastructure has been created all over the State by setting up as many as 44 tourist complexes providing numerous facilities like catering, accommodation (777 rooms), filling stations, lakes/bath complexes, landscaped gardens/fast food joints, shopping complexes, etc. This is a tremendous jump forward, indeed, that has gloriously brought the name of this tiny State on the tourist map of India.

Haryana has adopted a three pronged strategy for tourism promotion:[20]

(i) To Promote Highway Tourism

Haryana tourism has built tourist complexes at strategic points along the highways passing through the State.

(ii) To make Full Advantage of its Proximity to Delhi

Haryana tourism has developed tourist complexes around Delhi and other centres of tourist interest.

(iii) In the Third Part of its Strategy

Haryana tourism has provided tourist facilities at the district and sub-divisional headquarters to cater the needs of the local people.

The tourists complexes in Haryana have been imaginatively planned and carefully executed to meet the requirements of various kinds of tourists. The facilities available in the tourist complexes of Haryana ideally meet the requirements of both the affluent and the budget tourists.

7. Information Technology Infrastructure

With the introduction of information technology policy, Haryana state is now emerging as a counter magnet to Chennai, Bangalore and Hyderabad in the development of Information Technology. While lauding the significant role played by Haryana in achieving green revolution; now the state, through concerted efforts is going to make a name for itself in the field of Information Technology too. Efforts are also being made to make the state a top-ranking state in the field of software technology. At present, Haryana ranked third in the export of software in the country. A new project known as *"Nai Disha"* based on the system of district network is being launched to provide 20 types of web-enabled services to the people of Haryana besides generating employment opportunities. The project *"Nai Disha"* started in Panchkula on pilot basis is proposed to be implemented in all the districts of the state during the current financial year and next year. The main thrust of the Information Technology Policy (IT Policy) is to make information easily accessible to the public, to improve the quality of delivery of services to public, to improve the efficiency of the Government, to promote IT industry in the State, to create IT related jobs in the State, to promote IT education and literacy in the State and to promote IT infrastructure in the State. The State would soon become first in the country by computerizing all its treasuries and connecting them with the state treasury by December, 2003.

Information Technology Policy also lays emphasis on establishment of the communication backbone network for improving the telephony and internet connectivity in the state. For this purpose, the government has framed Right of Way (ROW) Policy and has signed agreements with two companies for laying optic fiber network in the state. The companies would also provide free bandwidth to the State Government for its usage. The facility would help the Government to establish a state-wise area network for the use of Government and providing services to citizens.

For efficient and transparent administration, the state Government also gives top priority to the use of information technology in the working of the Government Departments. The IT department has set-up a center for E-governance with various facilities. This center is proving useful in development of software and for imparting center has also provided computer training to all the Hon'ble Members of Haryana Legislative Assembly.

An Integrated Cyber City is being set-up at Gurgaon and it will provide employment opportunities to five lakh persons. To further improve the high speed communication, an earth station is being set-up at Gurgaon. The State Government is also exploring the possibility of setting up similar facilities at Panchkula. The state Government has decided to provide land for setting up a facility center of software technology park of India at Panchkula. Cyber cafes are being set-up in villages under *Gramodya Yojana*.[21]

IV. REGIONAL DISPARITIES IN INFRASTRUCTURAL FACILITIES

Economic welfare does not depends merely upon the level of development but on its distributive aspect also. Unfortunately the fruits of economic development is not equally distributed among different people and different parts of Haryana, causing disparities and imbalances in economic development in different regions. In this part of the chapter an attempt is made to analyse inter-district disparities from the view of infrastructural facilities in the state of Haryana. This analysis has been made in respect of three important components of Infrastructural facilities, namely:

(a) Roads,
(b) Railways, and
(c) Power.

(a) Roads

The total road length in the state was 5100 km. in 1966 which increased to 22,960 kms. in the year 1998-99. The road density in the state is depicted in Table 7.12.

The district-wise density of roads in Haryana in the year 2001 reveals that there are considerable disparities regarding the development of road network in various districts. A perusal of Table 7.12 brings to the light that out of 19 districts in the state 11 districts have density above state average while 8 districts are having density below state average. Panipat, Ambala, Panchkula, Yamuna Nagar, Kurukshetra, Gurgaon, Rewari have high density of roads,

TABLE 7.12

Density of Metalled Roads in Haryana (2001)

District	*Total Length*	*Area in sq. km.*	*Road Density (per 100 sq. km.)*
Ambala	1,093	1,574	69.44
Panchkula	560	898	12.36
Yamuna Nagar	1,083	1768	61.26
Kurukshetra	1,008	1,530	65.88
Kaithal	1,255	2,317	54.16
Karnal	1,101	2,538	43.38
Panipat	1,042	1,268	82.18
Sonipat	1,041	2,122	49.06
Rohtak	948	1,745	54.33
Jhajjar	885	1,834	48.26
Faridabad	1,209	2,151	56.21
Gurgaon	1,696	2,766	61.32
Rewari	984	1,582	62.20
Mahindragarh	945	1,859	50.83
Bhiwani	1,985	4,778	41.54
Jind	1,149	2,702	42.52
Hisar	1,851	3,983	46.47
Fatehabad	1,462	2,520	58.02
Sirsa	1,663	4,277	38.88
Haryana	22,960	44,212	51.93

Source: Engineer in Chief, PWD, B&R Branch, Haryana.

while Kaithal, Rohtak, Faridabad, Fatehabad were having medium density of metalled roads. The category of low density of metalled roads was confined to 8 districts, namely, Sonipat, Karnal, Jhajjar, Mahindragarh, Bhiwani, Jind, Hisar, Sirsa.

(b) Railways

Railways are called as life line of the Economy. In the

year 2000-01, the length of Railway lines in Haryana was 1451 kms. Ambala-Delhi is the railway line which carry most of the rail traffic in Haryana and it passes through the more developed parts of the state.

The district-wise analysis of rail route length indicates disparities in railway network as depicted in Table 7.13.

TABLE 7.13

District-wise Length of Railway Route in Haryana (2001)

District	*Total Length of Railway Lines (kms.)*	*Railway Route Density (per 100 sq. km. of area)*
Ambala	64.50	4.09
Panchkula	20.50	2.28
Yamuna Nagar	26.00	1.47
Kurukshetra	58.50	3.82
Kaithal	45.50	1.96
Karnal	60.80	2.39
Panipat	52.20	4.11
Sonipat	53.00	2.49
Rohtak	92.50	5.30
Jhajjar	18.20	0.99
Faridabad	71.50	3.32
Gurgaon	59.15	2.13
Rewari	128.60	8.12
Mahindragarh	100.75	5.41
Bhiwani	120.20	2.51
Jind	149.50	5.53
Hisar	159.50	4.01
Fatehabad	63.00	2.5
Sirsa	89.50	2.09
Haryana	1451.20	3.28

Source: General Manager (Statistics), Northern Railway, New Delhi.

A review of Table 7.13 reveals that railway route length per hundred sq. km. of area ranges from 0.99 to 8.12 km. indicating wide disparities in various districts. However, to some extent it is natural because density of railway line increases in those areas which exist in close proximity with railway lines connecting important railway stations of the state and nearby areas like Delhi, Punjab and J & K.

(c) Power

Power constitutes one of the most important element of infrastructure. Development of all the segments of the economy is inextricably linked with the development of power. Moreover, it reflects the level of standard of living also as the rate of consumption of electricity increases with the upliftment of standard of living. The disparities in district-wise consumption of electricity in Haryana is presented in Table 7.14.

A perusal of Table 7.14 indicates that 50% of power consumption is centralized only in two districts of Haryana, i.e. Faridabad and Gurgaon and remaining 50% is consumed by 17 districts of the state. Such vast disparities exists on account of highly industrialized economy, modernised housing and electrified roads in Faridabad and Gurgaon. There are three other districts, namely, Sonipat, Panipat and Hisar each of each share approximately 8% of total consumption. An important inference can be drawn from this information that there is vast scope of industrial development and economic upliftment in other districts of Haryana in order to bring them at par with these developed districts.

It is true that infrastructural facilities can not be at par in all districts or regions of the state because there is close relationship between economic development *vis-a-vis* infrastructural facilities. The only point to be considered is that in future those districts should be given preference in development of such facilities which are lagging behind at present. It will not only help in controlling over concentration of industrial units only in selected districts, but will also contribute significantly in balanced all around development of the state.

In the end we can say that Haryana is a pioneer state

TABLE 7.14

District-wise Consumption of Electricity in Haryana (2001)

District	*Consumption of Electricity (lakh k.w.h.)*	*Percentage share in total*
Ambala	3,154.66	3.11
Panchkula	1,389.67	1.37
Yamuna Nagar	3,529.97	3.48
Kurukshetra	233.30	0.23
Kaithal	223.16	0.22
Karnal	2,333.03	2.30
Panipat	8,064.17	7.95
Sonipat	8,571.34	8.45
Rohtak	4,818.21	4.75
Jhajjar	2,383.74	2.35
Faridabad	33,615.94	33.14
Gurgaon	16,341.36	16.11
Rewari	1,927.28	1.90
Mahindragarh	1,491.11	1.47
Bhiwani	2,769.20	2.73
Jind	497.03	0.49
Hisar	7,556.99	7.45
Fatehabad	547.75	0.54
Sirsa	1,988.14	1.96
Haryana	1,01,436.16	100.00

Source: Haryana Vidyut Prasaran Nigam Ltd.

as far as infrastructural facilities are concerned. The Haryana Government is progressively working for improvement of infrastructural facilities in the state, so that it becomes a model state for infrastructural facilities but it may be mentioned here that certain deficiencies still exist in infrastructural facilities and the following areas still need immediate government attention.

(A) Several initiatives have been made to attract

private investment in infrastructure development. There has been some success with increase in private participation in telecommunications, education, medical facilities, roads, etc. but the potential has not been fully exploited. A major problem coming in the way of private sector participation is the rationalisation of user charges, with many infrastructure sectors suffering from the levy of inadequate user charges. Bankable investments cannot be made in infrastructure unless they can be financed by the levy and collection of appropriate user charges. However, these have to be affordable so that the infrastructure service is used adequately. In fact, there is no difficulty in attracting private investment in areas such as telecom, roads, etc. where there are adequate returns on investment. The establishment of regulatory framework is also very critical for encouraging private investment in infrastructure sector. A regulator that is fair to consumers and sensitive to the needs of investors is absolutely necessary for infrastructure development.

(B) The power sector continues to face deficiencies even though the regulatory reforms process has been initiated through establishment of HVPN (Haryana Vidyut Prasaran Nigam Limited). The sector has not been able to attract private investment because of the financial unviability of State Electricity Board. There is urgent need to implement the much delayed power sector reforms, such as rational tariff-fixation, reduction in theft and transmission and distribution losses. Progress in such reforms would help in reducing gap between the cost of supply and revenue realised per unit of electricity generated. Only then will the generation and distribution of power became economically viable while reforming the power sector it must be ensured that needs of the rural sector are met, by making universal service obligations a part of reform process.

(C) Improvement in the transport infrastructure of the state will be essential for the achievement of accelerated growth of State Domestic Product (SDP) in the coming years. Major acceleration in SDP growth will imply faster growth in industry in particular. Such growth will place heavy demands on the transport sector. In the context of an increasingly competitive environment for manufactured goods the cost incurred in transportation has a significant bearing on the competitiveness of industrial goods in the national and international market. Thus, the supply of transportation services has to be improved and made more efficient in its entirety.

(D) The launch of the National Highway Development program at various level has provided a new radical thrust to the modernization and expansion of roads in the state. The resources for development of roads in the state can be further leveraged through the levy of affordable tolls on the road network. Haryana government has recently improved toll rates under the National Highway Development Programme. With the progress in the implementation of these programmes, the state can look forward to a modern road network within the next few years.

Notes and References

1. M.S. Patwardhan: Challenge and Opportunity for Industry, Commerce Annual number (1980), Vol. 141, p. 13.
2. S.M. Shah (1980): Technology for Strengthening Rural Base, Commerce Annual Number, Vol. 141, p. 23.
3. V.K.R.V. Rao (1980): Infrastructure and Economic Development, Commerce Annual Number, Vol. 141, pp. 9-10.
4. *Ibid.*
5. Statistical Abstract of Haryana (2000-01), p. 431.
6. Economic Survey of Haryana, 2001-02.
7. *Ibid.*, p. 27.
8. Quoted by K.L. Gupta: Economic Problems of India (2001), p. 1.

9. Wilfred Owen: Transportation and Development, *Journal of Transport Management*, July 1989.
10. Quoted by K.L. Gupta: Economic Problems of India (2000), p. 13.
11. Economic Survey of Haryana, 2001-02, p. 35.
12. *Ibid.*
13. Economic Survey of Haryana, 2003-04, p. 49.
14. Economic Survey of Haryana, 2001-02, p. 39.
15. General Manager, Indian Railways, Ambala Division.
16. Economic Survey of Haryana, 2001-02, p. 61.
17. *Ibid.*, p. 63.
18. *Ibid.*, p. 31
19. *Ibid.*, p. 30
20. *Ibid.*, p. 39.
21. *Ibid.*, pp. 51-52.

8

THE PATH AHEAD

Since its inception, the strong, simple, hard working and patriotic people of Haryana have been doing their best to make Haryana a model state of the country in every field of economic development. Haryana has marched towards modernity with leaps and bounds. It has during its brief span as an independent state in its own right, has done well. Much more, however needs to be done. Some of the assertions given below are noteworthy:

(A) The agriculture growth in the state has been remarkable, yet large accumulation of rice and wheat stocks, alongwith distinct shift in the consumption pattern away from cereals to non-cereals is a stark reminder that the policy focus needs to be reoriented towards the growth of non-cereal crops, i.e. oil seeds, pulses, fruits, vegetables and dairying. Diversification of agricultural production requires development of rural infrastructure, i.e. transportation, rural roads improved and reliable power supply, watershed management, cold storage, quality testing labs and institutional support by way of new market facilities, removal of restriction on stock limits and agricultural product movements. Agriculture research and extension would also require reorientation to meet the changing needs of the agriculture sector. Emphasis on minimum price support which has benefited only rice and wheat crops at the expense of other crops and agricultural products requires a fresh policy focus so that crop diversification gains momentum.

(B) Location of industry in Haryana is very lop sided. Almost 2/3rd of industry is concentrated in the districts which have proximity to Delhi or have proximity to State Capital Chandigarh. The reason for this lop sided growth is that industry always tend to locate itself in the region where it find ready market for its produce and raw material is easily available. The state government should come forward to remove this imbalance in location of industry. For this government should provide incentives and facilities for setting up the industrial units in backward areas of the state. Haryana government is making serious attempt in this regard but still there is lot to be done.

(C) Haryana has many advantages, major one being its close proximity to metropolitan Delhi, which enables it to provide any number of ideal location for all types and varieties of industries. The state has a healthy atmosphere of Industrial peace and amicable labour management relation. In view of all this, government should make an earnest effort to attract able entrepreneurs not only from other parts of the country but also from abroad for setting up industries in the state. Hon'ble Chief Minister Mr. O.P. Chautala has visited many foreign countries for attracting foreign investment to the state. Moreover, in the light of global competition facing industry today, the endeavour should be that industry in Haryana must continue to strive to be an efficient and competitive one and able to stand on its own in the face of rising domestic and foreign competition. In order to ensure this government on its part must ensure removal of remaining infrastructural constraints especially in power, transport and telecommunications, reducing bureaucratic controls in all spheres and removing all other barriers to the growth.

(D) Haryana is a pioneer state as far as infrastructural facilities are concerned. The Haryana Government is progressively working for improvement of infrastructural facilities in the state so that it becomes a model state for infrastructural facilities but still, following steps will go a long way in further development of infrastructural facilities.

(i) Development of efficient, low cost quality infrastructure services require high upfront cost and long gestation period. The need for huge investments necessitate the private participation. Government of Haryana has taken several initiatives to attract private investment. There has been some success with increase in private participation in telecommunication, roads, etc. but the potential has not been fully exploited. Private investment can be encouraged only if adequate returns are assured on their investment. Levy of affordable user charges will go a long way in assuring adequate returns to the private investors.

(ii) There are some infrastructural areas where there are large gaps between demand and supply and the private sector cannot be expected to step in significantly, e.g. rural infrastructural. In these sectors it is the responsibility of state government to ensure proper infrastructural facilities.

(iii) The power sector continues to face deficiencies even though regulatory reforms process has been initiated through establishment of HVPN (Haryana Vidyut Parsaran Nigam Ltd.). Following steps are needed in this regard:

(a) Private sector participation in power generation, transmission and distribution should be encouraged.

(b) There should be segregation of power generation, transmission and distribution function.

(c) Rational tariff fixation is must to make power sector self-reliant.

(d) Reduction in theft and transmission and distribution losses can be ensured through creation of independent power regulatory mechanism.

(iv) Improvement in transport facilities in the state is essential for achievement of accelerated growth. Government of Haryana had laid emphasis on modernization and expansion of road network in

Achievement of the goals of education for all and health for all not only involves a mix of public-private partnership in the provision of services but also a scaling down of the existing levels of subsidy to higher education and non-basic health facilities, and cost recovery in these public services from those in a position to pay. User charges would give a sound financial foundation to the provision of health and educational services and reduce the vulnerability of service delivery to public finances. Harnessing the private sector and N.G.O.'s for actual provision of services would improve the cost efficiency of production of these services. At the same time the delivery of health and education services must be ensured to those who cannot pay user charges.

In the end, it may be said that from a relatively backward and predominantly agricultural state at the time of its formation in 1966, Haryana has steadily risen to its pre-eminent position in all the spheres of economic development. This has been achieved largely because of a number of favourable factors, e.g. excellent law and order situation, an industrial relations climate conducive to development, an extensive road and communication network, total electrification, skilled and dedicated manpower and sizable disposable incomes generated by the rapidly rising production in all sectors of the economy, notably agriculture. Additionally and most importantly, Haryana enjoys certain significant natural advantages. Its geographical location with easy and inexpensive access to domestic consumer markets as well as export outlets, reliable water supply and availability of suitable land for industrial use make Haryana an ideal location for industry. Its relatively small size has been turned into another great advantage with an efficient and responsive administration which ensures minimum of red-tapism and bureaucratic interference. The rate of economic growth has been quite satisfactory and structural changes, to a great extent, indicate the movement of economy from developing to developed stage. However, there are certain limitations related to high growth of population and unbalanced development of certain areas. It is a matter of satisfaction that Haryana government is fully conscious of all these and if the suggestive framework evolved in this book is duly considered and incorporated in future planning of the state. Haryana will be one of the pioneer states of the country to gain the status of forward looking advanced Economy based on balanced and sound combination of different segments of economic activities.

APPENDIX I

HARYANA—AN ERA OF PROSPERITY[1]

Greetings to the people of Haryana on the Haryana Day. This day holds great significance of Haryana as it was on this day in 1966, it was carved out as a separate political entity. Every year this day inspires us and infuses amongst us an urge to make our contribution for the development of Haryana. Since ancient times, Haryana has remained a focal point in the political, social and religious spheres of the country. The brave soldiers of the land of the *Gita* have made supreme sacrifices in the freedom struggle of the country. This was the reason that the British neglected it and made it a backward area. Haryana could not attain an accelerated pace of development in the areas of economic, social and educational development after freedom of the country. Therefore, Jan Nayak Ch. Devi Lal launched a long and relentless struggle against such a step-motherly treatment meted out to the people of Haryana and played a vital role in making Haryana a separate political entity of the Indian Union. It is because of the effective implementation of the policies and programmes initiated by Jan Nayak Ch. Devi Lal that today an atmosphere of accelerated development with peace prevails in the state. Today, Haryana is humming with activity. The State has become synonymous to development by following the policies of Jan Nayak Ch. Devi Lal. Ch. Devi Lal had guided us till his last breath and the people of Haryana are proud of this son of the soil. The installation of the statue of Jan Nayak Ch. Devi Lal in Parliament House has made each Haryanvi proud as it signifies the contribution

---

1. Sh. O.P. Chautala, Hon'ble Chief Minister Haryana on Haryana Day, Nov. 1, 2003.

made by the Jan Nayak and the people of Haryana in per rapid development of the country. While implementing the policies and programmes for the welfare of the people, the present Government has taken a number of steps to ensure their participation so that the benefits of various schemes and programmes must also percolate to the grass root level. The dictum of Ch. Devi Lal, *"Bijli Pani Ka Prabandh Bharshtachar Bandh"*, is being followed in letter and spirit. I had held the reins of the administration about four years ago with the smallest ever 10-member Cabinet in the history of the country as a result of the mandate given by the people of the state. As I have the same spirit to fight for rights of the people as Jan Nayak Ch. Devi Lal had, I not only provided political stability also made the people understand high values of life in politics. I owe the credit of setting new trends and milestones in the development of State to the whole-hearted cooperation of the hardy people of the State. Immediately after assuming office, emphasis was laid on restoring the law of the land. Corruption has been checked with firm hand and the concept of good governance has been implemented in letter and spirit by providing clean and transparent Administration. The Government of India has appreciated our redressal system of public grievances by describing it as an ideal system. The present Government has introduced Industrial Policy, the formation Technology Policy, Education Policy and Sports Policy give a new orientation to these sectors. These policies have started yielding very encouraging results. The popular programme of *'Sarkar Aapke Dwar'* has given a new direction to the process of development in the State. The completion of about 40,000 developmental works under this programme to fulfil the aspirations of the people is itself a unique record. Agriculture is the mainstay of our Economic. A number of steps have been initiated to raise the socio-economic status of the farming communities. The rate of interest on cooperative loans has been reduced by four per cent. An action plan has been introduced for diversification of crops. A programme to plant medicinal plants would be planted on panchayat lands of 175 villages in each district. The State government has not only procured each grain of wheat, paddy and mustard, but also procuring bajra for the first time in the history of the State at a minimum support price of Rs. 505 per quintal. Haryana ranks first in the country in the export of basmati rice. The farmers have been given Rs. 110 per quintal for sugarcane and this is the highest price ever in the world. The cooperative sugar mills have cleared all arrears of the farmers and not even a single penny is to be paid to them now. The National Crop Insurance Scheme is also being implemented in the State. Haryana is known for its rich livestock. This year; the festival of *Gopashtmi* is also being celebrated on November 1. It is our tradition to worship even the cows and bullocks on this day Ch. Devi Lal has also great liking for the livestock and by following his ideals, to State Government has already given a grant of Rs. 5.63 crore to registered *'Gaushalas'* so as to improve their financial position. Grant of Rs. one crore is also being given to the *'Gaushalas'* today, i.e Government has also introduced an innovative insurance scheme for cows buffaloes and bullocks. The Haryana Government committed to make Haryana Denmark of India in the field of bulk production. Steps are being taken to provide modern medicare facilities for the cattle. A special campaign is being launched from today to repair veterinary institutions in the State. Wherever new 53 veterinary institutions are required, these would be set-up even by relaxing norms. The vacancies of the Animal Husbandry department would also be filled up on priority basis. The State Government is keen to provide all those facilities to the people in of rural areas as are available in urban areas. Therefore, a decision has been taken to set-up well-planned residential colonies in villages on the pattern of residential sectors in urban areas. This scheme is being launched from Uchana in Karnal district. Another campaign has been launched to construct community latrines for women in rural areas. The Haryana Rural Development Administration Fund Board has released Rs. 571 crore for implementation of various rural development schemes. The supply of safe drinking water has been accelerated in 2478 villages. Power being the pivot of development, the present Government has taken a number of steps to strengthen its generation, transmission and distribution systems. The installed capacity of power has been increased by 802 MW by the present Government. It is two-and-a-half times more than the increase made in power generation capacity by the two previous Governments during their tenure. At present, the rural sector is getting 55 per cent more power as compared to the year 1998-99. About 30,000 new tubewell connections have been released and this number is twice the number of tubewell connections released by previous two Governments. The sixth unit of Tau Devi Lal Thermal Plant, Panipat has been completed and now the work is in progress to set-up its seventh and eighth Units of 250 MW each. While the seventh unit would be completed in October next, the eighth unit would be completed in February 2005. The work to set-up 500 MW thermal power plant at Yamuna Nagar has also been taken up. As a result of these efforts, the State would not only be self-sufficient in power generation, but also able to supply it to the deficit States. Sutlej-Yamuna Link (SYL) canal is the lifeline of Haryana. Concerted efforts are being made to get Haryana's share of Ravi-Beas waters through this canal. The State Government has urged the Supreme Court to direct the Government of India to get the remaining portion of SYL canal completed through the Border Roads Organisation. The Government has implemented many irrigation schemes for optimum utilisation of each drop of water. The supply of irrigation water to four southern districts of Mahendergarh, Rewari, Bhiwani and Jhajjar has been increased by 25 per cent so as to safeguard the interests of the farming community: A Rs. 39.46 crore Bhakhra Canal Command Project is also being launched today. It would be the biggest ever project taken up by Command Area Development Authority of Haryana and cover 2.39 lakh hectares of area. The project has been sanctioned by the Union Ministry of Water Resources. Under this ambitious project, 1233 water courses falling in eight districts of Kurukshetra, Karnal, Kaithal, Fatehabad, Sirsa, Hisar, Ambala and Jind would be lined. Other on-farm-development schemes like installation of tubewells, underground pipe lines, sprinklers sets and drip irrigation would also be carried out by providing subsidy to small and marginal farmers under the project. The irrigation potential will also increase from 62 per cent to 87 per cent.

programme, all the 2.10 crore citizens of the State would be medically examined free of cost at their doorstep. Also, spectacles would be provided free of cost to those above 60 years of age.

A new scheme known as DEVIRUPAK has been introduced to check escalating population and growing discrimination between a boy and a girl. About 3100 couples have been registered so far under this scheme. A new sports culture has been created in the State as a result of the introduction of new Sports Policy. The sportspersons, who win medals at national and international meets are given cash awards ranging from Rs. 20,000 to Rs. one crore. A Regional Centre of Sports Authority of India, named after Ch. Devi Lal, is being set-up at Joshi Chauhan in Sonipat district. Unemployed Olympians are being given a monthly pension of Rs. 2000 and jobs have been reserved for outstanding sportsperson.

The Government has regularized the services of temporary, contractual and daily wagers. Today, Haryana is emerging as a fast developing State in the country. I am sure, the State would scale new heights of development in the near future as a result of the whole-hearted cooperation of the people. Let us pledge to dedicate ourselves to make Haryana the most prosperous State in the country.

BIBLIOGRAPHY

A. Books

Alagh, K., *Indian Development Planning and Policy—A Re-evaluation*, Vikas, New Delhi (1995).

Bhalla, G.S., *Changing Structure of Agriculture in Haryana: A Study of Impact of Green Revolution*, Economic and Statistical Organisation, Planning Department, Govt. of Haryana.

Bhattacharaya, S.N., *Industrial Potential Survey—Its Nature and Progress in Developing Economies.*

Bryce, D. Murra, *Industrial Development.*

Cassen, R.H., *India, Population, Economy and Society*, MacMillan, Delhi, 1979.

Chamola, S.D., *Agriculture Development Project for Haryana*, CCS, HAU, Hasar, 1999.

Chandri, M.K., *Trends of Socio-Economic Changes in India.*

Chennery, Hollis, *Redistribution with Growth*, Oxford University Press, London.

Clark, Colin, *The Condition of Economic Progress*, 1957.

Coale and Hoover, *Population Growth and Economic Development in Low Income Countries*, Princeton University Press, 1958.

Dernberg, T.C. and McDougall, D.M., *Macro-Economics*, McGraw Hill Book Company.

Dhar, P.N. and Lydail, H.F., *The Role of Small Enterprises in Indian Economic Development*, Delhi, 1962.

Dhar, P.K., *Indian Economy—Its Growing Dimensions*, Kalyani Publishers, New Delhi, 2001.

Dutt and Sundhram, *Indian Economy*, S. Chand & Company, New Delhi, 2001.

Fisher, A.G.B., *Economic Progress and Social Security*, 1945.

Ghatak, Subrata and Ingersent, Ken, *Agriculture and Economic Development*, New Delhi, 1984.

Gosal, G.S. and Krishan, *Regional Disparities in the Levels of Socio-Economic Development in Punjab*, PECO Printing Press, Chandigarh.

Gupta, K.L., *Indian Economy: Development, Problem and Planning*, Navyug Sahitya Sadan, Agra, 2001.

———, *Economic Problems of India* (2000), Navyug Sahitya Sadan, Agra, 2001.

Gupta, D.P., *Agricultural Development in Haryana*, Agricole Publishing Academy, 1993.

Gupta, S.R., *Haryana on the Road of Prosperity*, S.P. Publication, Mani Majra, Chandigarh, 1999.

Gupta, S.P., *Three Decades of Haryana*, S.P. Publication, Mani Majra, Chandigarh, 1999.

Hirschman, Albert O., *The Strategy of Economic Development*, Yale University Press, London.

Johar, R.S. and Rao, J.S., *Reflections in the Development of Punjab and Haryana.*

Kaur, K., *Structure of Industries in India—Pattern, Framework—Disparities*, Deep & Deep Publications, New Delhi, 1982.

Khan, N.A., *Problems of Growth of Under-developed Economy.*

Krishan Maharaj, *Tarik-Ki-Zillah*, Rohtak.

Kulkarni, M.R., *Industrial Development*, National Book Trust, New Delhi, 1971.

Kumar, Narinder, *Disparities in Level of Industrial Development of Haryana.*

Kuznets, Simon, *Six Lectures on Economic Growth*, 1966.

Kuznets, Simon, *Modern Economic Growth.*

Lal, Munni, *Haryana on High Road to Prosperity*, Vikas Publishing House Private Limited, Delhi, 1987.

Leon, C. Megginson, *Personnel and Human Administration*, Illinois, 1997.

Lewis, Arthur, *The History of Economic Growth*, Allen and Unwin, 1965.

Mahalanobis, P.C., *The Approach of Operational Research to Planning in India*, Asia, Bombay.

Mahajan, O.P., *Economic Growth in Haryana*, 1982.

Meir, G.M., *Leading Issues in Economic Development*, Oxford, University Press, Delhi.

Mishra and Puri, *Indian Economy.*

Madan, S., *Changes in Occupational Pattern and Industrialization in Haryana.*

Rao, V.K.R.V., *India's National Income.*

Rao, Lak Shmana V., *Economic Development of Andhra Pradesh,* B.R. Publishing Corporation, New Delhi.

Rao, P. Subba, *Essentials of Human Resource Management and Industrial Relations,* Himalaya Publishing Houses, Delhi.

Sagwan, N., *Development Process in Newly Organized State Haryana,* 1991

Sharma, R.K., *Technical Change, Income Distribution and Rural Poverty,* Shipra Publication, Delhi.

Singh, Jasbir, *Agricultural Geography of Haryana,* Vishal Publications, Delhi, 1987.

Singh, Jasbir, *Determinants of Agricultural Productivity,* Vishal Publications, Delhi, 1985.

Singh, Pritam, *Emerging Pattern in Puniab Economy,* Sterling Publishers Private Limited, New Delhi.

Todaro, Michael P., *Economic Development in Third World,* Orient Longman Ltd., Hyderabad, 1993.

Vepa, K. Ram, *Modern Small Industry in Indian Problems and Prospects,* Sage, New Delhi.

Verma, D.C., *Haryana.*

B. Periodicals

Adam, Curl, "Some Aspects of Educational Planning in Under-developed Areas", *Harvard Business Review,* Vol. 32.

Dadibavi, R.V., "Why these Inter-state Disparities", *Yojana,* Vol. 31, No. 11, June 16-30.

Dandekar, V.M. "Population front of India's Economic Development", *Economic and Political Weekly,* April 23, 1988.

Dhaiya, Bhagwan S., "Socio-Economic Disparities in Haryana", *K.U. Research Journal.*

Dhaiya, Krishna, "Growth of Service Sector in Haryana", *K.U. Research Journal.*

Dutt, Ruddar, "National Income, Inter State Variations", *The Economic Times,* May 11, 1986.

Gandhi, P., "Industrialisation, Infrastructure and Government

Policy in Haryana", *K.U. Research Journal*, 1991.

Gupta, D.D., Malik, H.S., Singh, V.K., "The Green Revolution and Imbalances of Cropping Pattern and Production Patterns of Crops in Haryana", *The Green Revolution a Symposium*, Harman Publishers, New Delhi.

Gulati, S.C., "Dimension of Inter-District Disparities", *Indian Journal of Regional Science*, Vol. IX, No. 2. 1993.

Joshi, B.M., "Inter-state Disparities and Economic Development", *Yojana*, Vol. 31, March 1987.

Johar R.S. and Singh, Parminder, "Regional Disparities in Agricultural Productivity in Punjab and Haryana—A Comparative Study", Punjab School of Economics, GNDU, Amritsar. 1991

Kaur, Kulwinder, "A Factor Analysis of Inter Regional Disparities in Industrialization—The Case of Haryana", *Margin*, Vol. 16, Oct. 1983.

Kuznet, Simon, "Economic Growth and Inequality", *American Economic Review*, March 1955.

Kundu Amitabh, K. Mahesh, "Variations in Sex Ratio, Development, Implications," *Economic and Political Weekly*, XXVI, No. 41.

Kumar, Anil, "Relationship between Macro-economic Variables and Growth of Industrial Sector in Haryana", Udyog Yug, August 2002.

Mazumdar, K., "Interstate Disparities in Per Capita State Domestic Product in India 1960-61 to 1985-86", *Indian Journal of Regional Science*, Vol. XXV, No. 1, 1993.

Mitra, Ashok "From Biological Reproduction to Social Reproduction", *Yojana*, Vol. 36, August 1992.

Mahajan, O.P., "Economic Growth in Haryana", *Journal of Haryana Studies*, Vol. XIV.

Patwardhan, M.S. "Challenge and Opportunity for Industry", *Commerce Annual Number*, Vol. 141, 1980.

Paul, Mohinder, "Industrialization and Economic Growth", *K.U. Research Journal*, 1997.

———, "Haryana: Demography and Economic Development", *Journal of Haryana Studies*, 1982.

———, and Chandra, Ballabh, "Inter-District Variation in Agriculture Growth, Productivity and Farm Income in Haryana", *Kautilya*, Vol. 11, 1994.

Rao, V.K.R.V., "Infrastructure and Economic Development", *Commerce Annual Number*, 1980.

Rao, V.K.R.V., "Changing Structure of Indian Economy as seen through National Accounts Data", *Economic and Political Weekly*, Dec. 15, 1979.

Shah, S.M., "Technology for Strengthening Rural Areas", *Commerce*, Annual Number 1980.

Singh, Jasbir "A New Technique for Measuring Agricultural Productivity in Haryana", *The Geographer*, Vol. 19.

Tomar, B.S., Singh, Arjun and Singh, Dalbir, "Growth of Education in Haryana", *Journal of Research*, HAU.

Yadav, K.C., "Impact of Green Revolution in Social, Economic and Political Life in Haryana", *K.U. Research Journal.*

Wilfred, Owen, "Transportation and Development", *Journal of Transport Management*, 1989.

World Bank, *World Development Report*, 1993.

C. Government Publications

Govt. of India, "Indian Economic Survey", Annual Publication.

Economic and Statistical Organisation, Planning Department, Haryana "Statistical Abstract of Haryana", Annual Publication from 1991-92 to 2001-02.

Director, Public Relations, Haryana "District Ambala—An Introduction."

Director, Public Relations, Haryana "District Kaithal—An Introduction."

Director, Public Relations, Haryana "District Mahindragarh—An Introduction."

Director, Public Relations, Haryana "Profile of District Jind."

Director, Public Relations, Haryana "प्रफुल्लित हरियाणा."

Director of Census Operation, Haryana "Population Total 2001."

Govt. of India, "Census of India—2001."

Govt. of India, "First Report of National Income Committee", April 1991.

Govt. of India, "National Family Health Survey."

Govt. of Punjab, "Statistical Abstract of Puniab" (1947-50), (1966).

Department of Agriculture Haryana, "Agricultural Statistics at a Glance—2001."

Economic and Statistical Advisor, Planning Department, Haryana, Economic Survey of Haryana, 2001-02.

Department of Industries, Haryana "Haryana for Industry—1997."

Department of Industries, Haryana, "Directory of Medium and Large Scale Industry—2001.

Department of Industries, Haryana, "Industrial Policy—1997."

Industrial Assistance Group, "Haryana for Industry—1996."

INDEX